"I love how Kevin takes 'happily ever after' tales and puts it back on my wife and me. And it's not always romantic, and it doesn't co but anyone can have it. Reading this book will help you get there.

—**Rossi Morreale**, TV personality

"Marriage is hard. Few do it well, and those who succeed need to have a ton of grace and a lot of wisdom. Kevin Thompson has modeled well what it means to have a marriage grounded in both wisdom and grace. This book is going to help a whole lot of marriages. Read it, practice it, and give it away!"

—**Brandon Cox**, pastor at Grace Hills Church;
editor of Pastors.com

"Kevin Thompson balances tried-and-true principles with a fresh perspective on the three main roles we have as spouses. Whether you're looking to strengthen or rescue your marriage, this book can help you determine where and how to make concrete improvements. Simple to read yet profound with insight, *Friends, Partners, and Lovers* is a book I'd encourage all married couples to pick up!"

—**J. Parker**, Christian intimacy author and speaker;
blogger at *Hot, Holy & Humorous*

"Kevin's book provides clear (and more importantly, doable) instruction for not only saving a broken marriage but also continuing to nurture a relationship that is healthy and happy. In a world where we watch people meet, fight, and break up via social media, his grounded advice is refreshing. I would absolutely and enthusiastically recommend *Friends, Partners, and Lovers* to my audience."

—**Kristan Roland**, blogger at *Confessions of a Cookbook Queen*

"With his sharp wit, a precise pen, wisdom beyond his years, and an ever-present posture of love, Kevin Thompson is a rare gift to the church. His writing carries a holy, transformational weight, and his readers are better for having spent time with his words."

—**Seth Haines**, author of *Coming Clean*

"It's not a mystery, but it is a challenge to create a healthy marriage. I appreciate Pastor Kevin's approach: keep it simple and be intentional about it. *Friends, Partners, and Lovers* is definitely a practical, thought-provoking, and timely message."

—**Rick Bezet**, lead pastor at New Life Church; author of *Be Real*

FRIENDS, PARTNERS, AND LOVERS

WHAT IT TAKES TO MAKE YOUR MARRIAGE WORK

KEVIN A. THOMPSON

Revell

a division of Baker Publishing Group
Grand Rapids, Michigan

© 2017 by Kevin A. Thompson

Published by Revell
a division of Baker Publishing Group
P.O. Box 6287, Grand Rapids, MI 49516-6287
www.revellbooks.com

Printed in the United States of America

Library of Congress Cataloging-in-Publication Data is on file at the Library of Congress, Washington, DC.

ISBN 978-0-8007-2811-3 (paper)

Scripture quotations are from The Holy Bible, English Standard Version® (ESV®), copyright © 2001 by Crossway, a publishing ministry of Good News Publishers. Used by permission. All rights reserved. ESV Text Edition: 2011

Published in association with William K. Jensen Literary Agency, 119 Bampton Court, Eugene, OR 97404.

17 18 19 20 21 22 23   7 6 5 4 3 2 1

In memory of Coy and Ella Vest,
whose seventy years of loving one another
was a form of loving me.

To Jenny.
This book is a feeble attempt
to help others experience
what you have given me.

Contents

Acknowledgments

I never set out to be a writer about relationships. A few years ago, I began www.kevinathompson.com with the intention of writing about leadership and current events. A few months in, I wrote an article about marriage, and the response was immediate. While other articles received attention, the topic of marriage found an audience. What began as happenstance became a weekly habit of writing about marriage. Much of this book is an overflow of that. The ideas found here were formed and tested on my website. As readers responded, questioned, and told me their stories, I became convinced of the need for this book. Without those readers and their willingness to share, like, interact, question, and encourage, this book would have never been. Thank you.

I would also like to thank:

Mom and Dad. There was never a day in which Leigh or I doubted your love. There were times in which I doubted Leigh's love, but it was probably the strongest of them all.

Bruce and Verna. You loved Jenny well, and I benefit from that every day.

Ed, Shara, and the co-workers both past and present I've spent the last fifteen years with, especially those who have been there for most of that time—Matt and Becca, Susan and Bart, Michelle and Mark. Your marriages make my marriage better.

The men who call me friend before they call me pastor and, in so doing, make me a better pastor—Jay, Michael, Dick, and many others.

Calvin Miller. Although he has left this earth, his teaching and friendship still sticks with me.

The leadership and membership of Community Bible Church. Your generosity and support never cease. You endured a teenager as he learned to communicate. You encouraged a twenty-something as he was becoming a man. And you have empowered a thirty-something to chase his dreams. I'm grateful.

Teresa Evenson and those at the William K. Jensen Literary Agency. I'm thankful our friend Seth Haines said we could trust one another.

Andrea Doering, Twila Bennett, and those at Revell. Thanks for patiently teaching me this process and pretending like my questions are normal.

Ella and Silas. I write, in part, so I can still talk to you after I'm gone.

Jenny. One of my favorite things is knowing there is nothing I can write here that will move you to tears, yet I try anyway. My greatest privilege in life is calling you mine. Thank you for choosing me in return. One of the reasons I'm so passionate about marriage is because of how fortunate I feel to have you. Thank you for every word you have edited, every story you have endured, and every time you've restrained yourself from quoting me back to me.

1

The Number One Cause of Divorce

Eugene and JoAnn were the oldest members of our church. They had been married for seventy years and were inseparable. Having never had children, they treated me like one of their own. As Eugene's health began to fade, our visits became more special. One day they dropped by my office to give me some banana bread they had made. Knowing our times together were limited, I dropped what I was doing and engaged them in conversation.

After a half hour, Eugene turned to JoAnn and said, "Well, are you going to give him the bread?" She looked confused and said, "Me? You brought the bread." After a terse back-and-forth, they realized they had left the bread on the kitchen counter. Being in better health, JoAnn drove back to their house to get it.

As she made the drive back, Eugene and I spoke with several co-workers who dropped by to see him. One asked, "Mr. Eugene, what's the key to being married seventy years?" Without hesitation, he said, "Tell her every day that you love her."

Minutes later JoAnn returned with the loaf of bread and a hint of frustration. Trying to mend fences between them, I asked, "JoAnn, what's the key to being married seventy years?" She quickly responded, "Tell him every day that you love him." Those in the office were awed by how swiftly they had given the same answer. They had what we all desired—a lifetime love proven over seven decades of dedication and commitment.

A few months later, Eugene was near death. One day I dropped by the hospital and JoAnn took that opportunity to run home and check on their dogs. With it being just the two of us, I was able to ask Eugene some serious questions about love and life. I recounted the story from my office and asked, "Tell her every day you love her—is that really the key to marriage?" He paused and then said, "Yep, that's the key—memorize her answers."

If only marriage was like a third grade spelling test—we could memorize our spouse's answers and be assured of a perfect life. But marriage isn't that easy. Eugene knew the truth, which allowed him to joke as though success in marriage was some trite act of memorization. Seventy years had taught him otherwise. He knew that marriage was far more complicated than a simple answer.

But he also knew that a successful marriage doesn't happen on a whim. It isn't a fortunate twist of fate. While marriage can't be drilled down to a simple formula, it does have a basic design. When we comprehend its structure, a happy marriage is far more likely.

Eugene and JoAnn symbolized what marriage could be. When we consider an elderly couple celebrating seventy years together, holding hands on the nursing home porch, many things come to mind. But one thing is never felt—pity. No one feels sorry for the couple who experienced only one love. Instead, we feel envy. We want what they have. As a pastor, I'm honored to know many couples whose love has lasted through every stage of life. But sadly, I regularly see the other side of marriage. I interact with people in broken marriages on a weekly basis. On most occasions, by the time those couples call me, the marriage is over. There is always a reason:

"He loved his work more than me."

"She just never let me in."

"The other relationship started innocently."

"He is so stingy with money."

"She was so ungrateful."

The list is endless. Nearly every person comes into my office with a reason why their relationship ended. Much of the time they blame the other party. Sometimes they are right; often they are wrong. On occasion, they take personal responsibility for what has happened.

Far more marriages die of apathy than adultery.

But rarely does a person properly diagnose the true reason for why the relationship didn't make it.

I'm convinced the number one cause of divorce is not adultery, financial problems, or irreconcilable differences. Those issues are real, and they might be the most pressing issues the couple feels as the relationship heads in a negative direction, but they are not the root cause.

The number one cause of divorce is a lack of intentional investment in the marriage. Far more marriages die of apathy than adultery. They end more from a failure of intention than a failure of finances. In nearly every instance in which a marriage ends, a couple or individual has failed to do the work necessary to make the marriage succeed. Rarely will they see their failure. They are far more likely to blame a reason other than the real source of the problem.

Why do so many marriages end because of a lack of intention? I believe it is due to one of these three reasons:

1. Some are lazy and don't want to do the work.
2. Some believe marriage is magic, so they shouldn't have to do the work.

3. Some are deceived into thinking marriage is a flip of a coin, so there is no use doing the work.

All three are dangerous mistakes.

Laziness Born of Fear

Some spouses refuse to make any serious effort at marriage. It's frustrating and confusing. Whenever a person says "I do," they are also saying "I will," but sadly, too many people say "I won't." They refuse to learn, grow, or understand. They demand much from their spouse but give nothing in return. They either know nothing of what it takes to make marriage flourish or simply refuse to do anything necessary for success.

While these characteristics likely reveal themselves during the dating process, the behaviors are often overlooked or justified. Although there are times when both spouses are lazy and refuse to make a marriage thrive, more often one spouse is willing while the other is not. There are few things more tragic than when one spouse desperately desires a marriage to succeed and the other is unwilling to make any effort. Maybe the couple got married without understanding what is necessary, and once they were married they regretted it. But more often, a person gets married and then gets scared. Laziness is often born of fear.

Afraid of what marriage demands of them, fearing they may not have what it takes, unwilling to admit weakness or failure, some spouses shut down. They feign apathy in hopes of masking their fear. And it works. Their spouse never sees their fear but quickly sees their apathy.

Marriage demands courage. It requires strength when we have none to give. It calls for transparency when we want to be secretive. We have to run toward problems when we want to run away. We have to admit fault when we want to deny. We have to recognize ignorance and do something about it. Where inaction feels easier in the moment, success in marriage requires us to regularly refuse immediate gratification in order to choose the hard road of discovery and growth. And some people refuse the road. Unfortunately, there is nothing a spouse can do if their husband or wife chooses the lazy way. As a husband, I can do many things, but one thing I cannot do is force my wife to care. Similarly, my wife cannot change my will.

But I can do that. It's an empowering feeling to understand the amount of control I have over myself. While I can't dictate my marriage, I can greatly influence it by controlling what I control—myself. As I work with intention on myself, the marriage is changed.

I Love You, but You Are Not My Soul Mate

The good news is that the lazy are not the norm. Far more often, couples do not put in the work because of one of two misconceptions. The first is that marriage doesn't require work because our spouse is perfect for us, and the second is that marriage is just based on luck. We long for the idea of a soul mate. We think every Adam has an Eve, every Romeo needs a Juliet, and every Kate Middleton has her Prince William. A good number of people believe that there is one perfect person who was created for them and that the great challenge of life is to find him or her. Until they do, they will have a second-rate life, but when they find that person, everything will be perfect.

This is the story most often told in Hollywood. It's romantic to watch two people struggle to find each other or to realize that they were meant to be together. And when they are, the music plays and the movie ends. Yet what we never see is that a few years after the storybook wedding, the perfect movie couple is struggling to make marriage work in the same way that every other couple struggles. Romantic comedies hit on a serious truth—we all want to experience meaningful love. However, they present that love in a false form—just find the right person and all will be well.

If soul mates existed, I would believe that Jenny is mine. I can't imagine someone better for me. Yet if Jenny and I weren't married, we would probably both be married to someone else. Jenny could have a happy, satisfying, and meaningful life with one of many different men. She has simply chosen me. She loves me, but I'm not her soul mate.

The idea of a soul mate comes from Greek mythology. Legend holds that the Greek god Zeus looked down on four-armed and four-legged humanity with fear. He was afraid we could become too powerful and might overtake him. In an effort to weaken us, he cut us in half so that we would spend our days searching for our twin soul—our soul mate, or our other half. It is from Greek mythology that some believe there is only one person created exactly for you. If the idea of a soul mate is true, then so are these:

Marriage should be easy. If someone was created just for me, we should fit together like a perfect glove. Every one of my weaknesses should be compensated by her strength, and each of my strengths should compensate for her weaknesses.

Not only would it be possible to marry the wrong person, but it would actually be likely. If there is just one person I can marry, the chances of me finding that person—especially on the first try—is slim. If I marry the wrong person, either I'm destined to failure or I need to divorce.

If I'm single, my life is not complete. If I'm looking for my other half, then I'm just half a person until I find them. In this line of thought, the single life is a second-class one that should be pitied.

However, all of these are lies. They interject stress into dating relationships, weaken marriages, and create discontent in anyone who believes them. The truth is that we have the choice to marry or not to marry. Either way, our lives are meaningful and complete. Chances are that our life satisfaction will be the same once we are married as it would be if we didn't marry at all. Marriage doesn't make life satisfying as much as it reveals how we already feel.

Knowing our spouse isn't our soul mate allows us to expect problems. We aren't surprised by frustrations. We understand differences. When we fight, it doesn't cause us to wonder if we married the wrong person. We know it is just part of marriage.

The great challenge of relationships is not to find the one person created specifically for you. It is to pick someone and work at the relationship to such an extent that eventually you feel as though there could never be anyone else for you.

My wife is not my soul mate. She does not complete me. As romantic as it sounds to say she was created for me, it is far more truthful to say she chose me. If soul mate mythology were true, love would not be a choice but an uncontrollable urge. But the truth is much more beautiful. My wife wasn't forced to love me; she has chosen to love me. She wasn't created for me; she has given herself to me. The idea of a soul mate might look more appealing on a card; it might feel more romantic in a movie.

> *The great challenge of relationships is not to find the one person created specifically for you. It is to pick someone and work at the relationship to such an extent that eventually you feel as though there could never be anyone else for you.*

But in truth, it is only a mirage of something far better—a truly committed relationship based on the individual choice of love.

Which is better, a love of choice or a love of force? I'm grateful my wife is not my soul mate. It reaffirms her true love for me. She was not forced to love me, but she has freely chosen to do so. Those who believe in a soul mate are tempted not to work at marriage, believing they don't have to because their spouse is made for them.

Marriage Is Not a Flip of a Coin

I hear it all the time: "Marriage is just a flip of a coin." Based on this "fact," an online writer made the case that being a swinger is an acceptable lifestyle and one that should not only be accepted but actually encouraged. It's depicted in television shows. I'm sure the writers think they are dictating absolute truth. Look around. Failure in marriage is everywhere, so anyone who has a good marriage just got lucky.

There is no doubt that a good marriage feels like luck. Jenny and I regularly discuss how lucky we feel. I see friends, talk with readers, and sit with those whose marriages are failing, and oftentimes it seems as though some people are just unlucky.

Not long ago, I received a phone call from a man who said the magic was gone from his marriage. He thought he had made a mistake. He didn't "feel it" anymore and thought he never could. "I guess I flipped the coin and lost," he said.

A girl does everything right, but a few years into marriage the guy cheats and the relationship ends. A guy lives radically differently from his friends and finds a great mate, but she refuses to grow up and the marriage dies. A young couple is the epitome of how a young couple should be, but within a decade they are not together anymore.

A good marriage can feel like luck because there are many people who have experienced the sting of divorce yet haven't done anything more wrong than the rest of us. They weren't perfect, but their mistakes should not have ended in a divorce. Still, their marriages dissolved and they are feeling the weight of trying to put their lives back together. Individuals can have bad fortune. They can be perfectly willing to do whatever is necessary to make a marriage work, but their spouse is not. Where one is unwilling, both suffer. To them, it feels like a flip of a coin.

Yet marriage isn't a flip of a coin; it's a flip of the will. Unless two people are willing to submit their individual wills to that which is best for the couple, a marriage will likely fail. While marriage might seem like a great mystery that is highly unpredictable, it is actually fairly simple to predict if a marriage will last. When a couple believes that marriage is a coin toss, they are tempted not to make any effort. Why put effort into something that may not work? Why not just keep flipping the coin until it comes up a winner?

Work Matters

The work of marriage matters in many areas, but it is most notable in our emotions. Couples rarely understand the extent to which they control their feelings toward their spouse. By intentionally investing in our marriage, our affection for our spouse will grow.

It's a reciprocal relationship with powerful implications:

We invest toward our affections.

Our affections go toward our investments.

Consider where you put your money. Few things reveal our heart as much as money. We give to those things that are important to us. There is likely a specific reason why you give to one charity and I give to another. Both likely do great work, but you are passionate about one. Why? Chances are you had some personal experience that gave rise to your passion. A mother had cancer so you give to fight breast cancer, or a child got sick so you give to St. Jude. I have a daughter with Down syndrome, so I often give money and time toward Special Olympics. Our resources can reveal our hearts.

> *Marriage isn't a flip of a coin; it's a flip of the will.*

Yet the reverse is also true. If you picked a stock out of the blue and invested $10,000 toward it, several things would happen. You would find yourself watching the stock price. Anytime a news story on that stock sector made headlines, your attention would

19

be drawn to it. You might even begin to research more about what that company does and what the future looks like for it. Your investment would influence your affection.

Healthy couples leverage this reciprocal relationship to the benefit of their marriage. First, they love one another, so they naturally invest in each other. They spend time together. They study one another. They notice what is taking place in their spouse's life. They invest because of their affections. They also invest in order to change their affections. They don't just wait until they feel something to do something. They form the discipline of doing things so they will feel. As they invest in their spouse (even when they don't feel like it), that investment influences their affections.

The most common statement I hear from couples who are divorcing is "I just don't love him/her anymore." Many couples even rewrite history to say they have never loved one another. What they fail to understand is that they have the choice of whom they love. They control their feelings. What most often happens when love is lost is that a couple lives in an apathetic season in their relationship. They stop intentionally investing in one another and the marriage, and over time the feelings of love wane. This pattern often happens when the chaos of parenting tempts a couple away from working on their marriage.

Brandon and Lana met in college. She caught his eye the first time he saw her. She was slower to warm up to him. Eventually he wore her down and she agreed to a date. One date led to another, and within a year they were engaged. Both partners were career driven, but family was of utmost importance. Three kids were born within their first eight years of marriage. Life for Brandon and Lana was chaotic but fun. As the kids got older, the family's schedule was demanding. They juggled two work schedules, multiple sports schedules each season, and the desire to travel on the rare weekends they were free.

No matter the day, there was always something on the schedule. Neither spouse noticed their feelings for the other fading. By the time Lana recognized it, she thought it was just the normal ebb and flow of married life. She wouldn't have done anything about it had she not met Mark. He was a colleague at work. Their families interacted on occasion. Lana knew Mark's wife, but they weren't close.

It began with simple conversation. He was thoughtful. He remembered small details and asked about them. Whereas Brandon would have to be reminded of the most obvious aspects of Lana's life, Mark noticed when she got a haircut or had new shoes or was worried about her mother's diagnosis.

Nothing had happened between the two, but Lana was in my office because she could see the direction the relationship was headed. The last thing she wanted to do was hurt Brandon or her kids or Mark's family, but she loved Mark. While she said she still loved Brandon, it was a cognitive love. She felt nothing for him. Now she was asking what she should do.

It wouldn't be easy, but the solution was simple. Lana needed to cut all communication with Mark and reinvest in her relationship with Brandon. It would take some time, but if she would intentionally reconnect with Brandon, all those old feelings would come flooding back. As a matter of fact, she could have many more feelings for Brandon than anyone else because he was a good dad to her kids, they had a long history together, and they knew each other unlike anyone else. Lana's feelings for Brandon were dead, but they could be resurrected. It was in her best interest (and everyone else's) to bring those feelings back rather than end two marriages and try a new relationship with Mark.

One of the greatest failings we will face as couples is not being aware of how much control we have over our emotions. Too often we see love as a force that overpowers us rather than a choice we make. We choose whom we love. Most often that choice is determined by our investment.

Consider any relationship. Two people find each other interesting. Clearly it doesn't begin as love. Maybe it's lust or infatuation or just interest, but it's not love. Yet they begin to spend time together. They go on dates, have conversations, and get to know each other. Over time, love grows, but it only grows because they have invested in each other. Without the dates, phone calls, and interactions, they would not have fallen in love.

Apathy will slowly erode a marriage, but intention will cause it to continually grow.

In the same way we fall in love, we stay in love. We invest in each other, which causes our affections to grow. If your marriage requires anything, it requires intention. To the extent that both spouses are intentional about keeping the marriage healthy, it will thrive. Apathy will slowly erode a marriage, but intention will cause it to continually grow.

Work *In* and *On*

When it comes to marriage, we work in two specific ways—both *in* and *on*. In his book *The E-Myth Revisited: Why Most Small Businesses Don't Work and What to Do about It,*[1] Michael Gerber makes a distinction between working *in* your business and working *on* it. His point is that for a business to grow, a leader must spend some time thinking about the big picture of how the company is operating. Too often a small business owner is so busy with the day-to-day operation of the business that they cannot do the necessary work to help it grow.

The same is true for marriage. For marriage to succeed, each spouse must be working *in* it. Money has to be made. Kids have to be raised. Bills have to be paid.

The to-do list of my average day—between work, marriage, parenting, civic duty, personal goals and aspirations, and a laundry

1. Michael Gerber, *The E-Myth Revisited: Why Most Small Businesses Don't Work and What to Do about It* (New York: HarperCollins, 2001).

list of other categories—can be overwhelming. It takes work, and oftentimes a lot of it, just to keep the household up and running. Yet it is still easy to feel like a continual failure. I've got to skip one meeting for another. I returned three phone calls but never got to the fourth. I helped my wife with a couple of things, but she could really use my help with another. Do I take a few moments to study with my children, or do they deserve some playtime? We don't have time for both.

It takes a lot of work *in* marriage just to get through a day. And many couples fail at this. Laziness destroys a marriage. Often a couple may remain together because the lazy spouse could never make it on their own and the working spouse is too busy to end the relationship. Yet a marriage with a lazy spouse is never healthy. (Note: Do not confuse "working" with "having a job." By "working" I mean someone expending mental, physical, and emotional energy to keep the family running. A lot of people have jobs but aren't working in their marriage.) Marriage takes so much effort from a day-to-day perspective that it is easy for a couple never to take time to consider the big picture. They get so busy that they cannot see past today in order to determine if they like the direction their marriage is headed. This is a recipe for disaster. A couple must take time to work *on* their marriage.

Finding the time can feel impossible. As parents are raising children, the idea of adding one more responsibility is overwhelming. Yet if a couple will intentionally set aside specific times to work *on* their marriage, they will be better able to work *in* their marriage.

Working *on* one's marriage does several things:

It re-creates a sense of partnership and togetherness.

It makes each spouse feel heard and respected.

It allows a couple to renegotiate responsibilities and expectations.

It provides a break from day-to-day demands.

It gives perspective and time to consider new possibilities.

It reminds the couple the world continues to go on even when they take time off.

It creates opportunities for growth and encouragement.

It reveals strengths to appreciate and weaknesses to improve within the relationship.

Working *on* the relationship is an important part of having a healthy marriage. Without intentional time to reflect, discuss, and plan how they will work *in* a marriage, a couple is left hoping things work out in a positive way rather than determining how they will make things work. There are several ways to work *on* a marriage, but there is one common key—intentional communication. This is what prevents most people from ever looking at the big picture. It is always easier in the moment to avoid intentional communication about the marriage and to simply run the kids to the next soccer game or discuss what you should eat for dinner.

It is far more difficult—and risky—to ask questions like these:

Are you happy in this relationship?

What am I not doing for you that you need me to do?

How am I making you feel used rather than valued?

Is the housework properly divided, in your opinion?

Do you feel your heart coming more alive or dying?

There is a host of other questions that can and should be discussed. Discussions like these do not have to happen every day or every month, but there should be some time in which an open dialogue can take place and each spouse has the ability to safely communicate how they feel. Working *in* a marriage is necessary, but working *on* the marriage is just as important.

Divorces seem to happen for a variety of reasons, but no matter the presenting symptom, nearly every failed marriage has died because one or both spouses have neglected to intentionally invest in it. Thankfully, the number one cause of divorce is completely avoidable. We can become aware of the danger and intentionally choose a different way. Intentional investment can become the number one cause of a successful marriage.

BE INTENTIONAL

1. Which is the greatest temptation you face regarding apathy in marriage—you don't want to work, you don't think you need to work, or you don't think your marriage is worth the effort?
2. When can you set aside time to work *on* your marriage?
3. How would you and your spouse answer the five difficult questions above?

2

People Stay in Love in Predictable Ways

I love to hear stories of how people first fell in love. Each one has a unique quality to it. For most, there was a minor moment that deeply changed the course of their history—a chance meeting, something that caught their eye, or an instant in which their heart skipped a beat. If they hadn't fallen in love, these moments would be long forgotten, but because a love developed, the moment is long remembered.

For me it was a touch. Jenny and I went on our first date in college. Before we went out, I went through my normal class schedule, which that semester included a class on human sexuality. I only remember two specific aspects of the class:

1. I was continually embarrassed as my five feet two, grandmotherly professor was far more open about human sexuality than anyone this naive boy had ever heard before.
2. In a dating relationship, if a woman is interested in the man, she will likely make the first touch. Watch for it, and if it happens, reciprocate the touch.

I remember the second point only because it was said the week Jenny and I were supposed to go out. The professor was lecturing about something and, as an offhanded comment, simply mentioned the importance of touch. To illustrate how touch can communicate, she mentioned how research had shown that on a first date women often make the first touch if they are interested in the other person. It isn't a conscious move, just a natural response to the closeness they are feeling. If that touch is reciprocated within a reasonable time frame, the relationship will move forward. If it is never offered or not reciprocated, the relationship will probably never develop.

I have no idea if this is true or not, but I do know that going into our first date I was waiting to see if Jenny would touch me. And she did.

After dinner as we were walking and talking, I said something playful and she gently hit my arm as she responded. To this day she said it meant nothing, but at the moment it meant everything to me. She touched me, which, according to the latest in human sexuality, meant she liked me, so I better touch her back. It took about five minutes, but I finally found my opportunity to gently make physical contact. And the rest is history.

> *What makes marriage work is predictable, universal, and completely under our control.*

Had we not gotten married, that touch would have meant very little. But because we did get married, I can still tell you exactly where we were the moment she touched my arm—in the toy aisle at Walmart in our college town.

We tend to think of love as a mystery, and the mystery of what makes us fall in love is fascinating. But staying in love is not mysterious. What makes marriage work is predictable, universal, and completely under our control.

People stay in love in very common ways:

Making the relationship a priority.

Being committed solely to one another.

Intentionally building their friendship with one another.

Continually growing as individuals and as a couple.

Assuming the best about one another and being worthy of receiving that assumption.

Being fair toward one another.

Understanding the power of little things, like saying "thank you" and "you're welcome."

Making an effort to know one another and continually growing in that knowledge.

Discussing any important issue, but always in the context of it being just one issue.

Choosing to act in love even when love isn't felt.

It sounds much cooler to talk about the mysteries of love. We like the idea that love is unexplainable, because if we can't explain it we can't be expected to maintain it or grow it.

Yet love doesn't work that way. It might begin as a mystery, but it continues in the mundane. What feels overwhelming is actually completely in our control as we choose whether or not we will live out our vows for a lifetime. The unconscious touch of a hand on a first date must become the very conscious touch of a hand in every day of marriage.

People stay in love in very predictable ways. This book is about those ways. What makes marriage work? What is my role as a husband? What does my wife need from me, and what do I need from her? What is the role of a spouse?

Before the Leaves

Marriage is not my invention. As unique as it felt when my wife and I fell in love, men and women had been experiencing the same

29

emotions for centuries before us. When we said "I do," we entered into an institution created long before we were born.

Culture and time clearly play a role in influencing the structure of marriage, but the foundational principles of what makes a marriage work are no different today than they have ever been. While each husband and wife must find their unique way of expressing the marriage covenant, the first step to a healthy marriage is discovering the original design of the relationship.

In Genesis 2, God created marriage. Before sin entered the world or humanity experienced shame, God created humans and designed us to need one another. From the Genesis 2 story, it is clear that man and woman are to play three distinct roles within their relationship.

Having created Adam, God declared it was not good for him to be alone. In order to show the perfection of the one he would create, God paraded every living creature before Adam and allowed him to name each one. Adam could see that while the creatures were good, none would make a good match for him. Something was missing.

When Eve was created, she was described as being a suitable fit for him. She could be something for Adam that nothing else could. By sharing his humanity, Eve could be a *friend*. She could give him a sense of companionship that no other creature could. While the other animals could be good company, the relationships between man and animal would always be subservient. Eve brought a unique equality to the relationship. Adam and Eve were different, yet the same. They had compatible strengths while sharing a common humanity. Theirs could be a friendship like no other.

Adam and Eve's companionship was meaningful in and of itself, but it also served another purpose. They were given a task. They were not just placed in the garden to exist; they were called to be caretakers of the garden. They were to function as *partners*. They would work together using their God-given talents to steward what God had created. While the other animals would play a role in that task, theirs was a unique partnership, and their success was dependent on their ability to work together.

Genesis 2 ends with a beautiful description of God's creation of humanity: "The man and his wife were both naked and were not ashamed" (v. 25). This physical condition served as a window into their emotional and spiritual connection. There was no division between the two, no sense of shame, no break in their intimacy. Their differences were not hidden but were fully exposed and celebrated. This shows the third role that Adam and Eve were to play for one another: *lovers.*

When God created Eve, he gave Adam a friend, partner, and lover all wrapped up in one person. Each role was not played in isolation but instead complemented the others. Friendship brought trust and understanding. Partnership brought meaning and fulfillment. Being a lover brought intimacy and connection.

This was God's design in creation. It was how things were before sin entered the world. This was marriage before the leaves. Yet when sin came, so did shame. Trust was lost. Working together became more difficult. Intimacy was shattered. As Adam and Eve adorned leaves in order to cover their shame, what had been created to be easy became difficult.

After the leaves, shame, blame, and insecurity were natural aspects of marriage. What was meant to come naturally now has to be discovered, learned, and fought for. Before sin, the first marriage needed no intention because Adam and Eve would function within their appropriate roles without thought. But after the leaves, everything changed.

We live after the leaves. In rare moments we can still sense the way marriage was supposed to be. We feel known, loved, connected, and adventurous, but those feelings quickly fade and give way to doubt, uncertainty, and fear.

Sin radically changed marriage, but it did not transform its basic design. It made marriage more difficult. It eliminated the guarantee of success. It ensured that even the best marriage would have moments of disappointment and seasons of struggle. But it did not change the roles we are supposed to play.

What changed was not the design but the effort it would take to live out the design. When sin entered the world, intention became a necessary prerequisite for a successful marriage. What would have happened naturally if sin were not present now requires great effort, struggle, the experience of failure, the need for forgiveness, the sharing of grace, and the strength to try and try again.

Sin radically changed marriage, but it did not transform its basic design.

Just as Adam and Eve were created to be friends, partners, and lovers, so too every couple who commits to live their lives solely with one another needs to play the same roles. We have to be intentional about discovering and experiencing God's design for marriage.

Three People You Married

I know I'm one person. I have one mind, one heart, one soul, and one body. But if you were to interview a good cross section of the people I interact with on a regular basis, you would likely get a variety of descriptions of me.

Some, having watched me on stage, would describe me as extremely extroverted, even while those who know me best would tell you I am an introvert. Some would say I'm cold and nearly emotionless, while others would say I'm a sap who has a difficult time not caving to people's demands. Some would say I'm a strong leader with clear vision, while others would say I might be many things, but a leader is not one of them.

Ask a hundred people to describe me and you would likely get four or five major descriptions with a multitude of minor variances. I'm one person, but I'm many people—husband, father, son, brother, speaker, writer, friend, opponent, citizen. Whenever we marry someone, we are marrying one person, but they are also many people. They have a variety of roles to fill, and we only see them in a select number of those roles.

Yet even within the dynamics of marriage, a person is not one person. They are three. While they might be stronger in one area than another, all three are vital to creating a healthy marriage and being a good partner.

As a spouse, I *must* be three people.

Friend

At the foundation of any good marriage is deep friendship. By no means should a spouse be your only friend, but they should be your best friend. Over the course of a marriage, spouses will spend a tremendous amount of time together and should enjoy being in the presence of one another. Deep levels of trust, admiration, and respect should define every marriage.

Many marriages struggle because they begin as a friendship, but the couple does not continue to develop the friendship through the marriage. They assume it will happen naturally, not realizing a healthy relationship requires intention and effort. Others make a grand mistake when they do not see friendship as an important aspect of who to marry. Saying you wouldn't want to ruin the friendship is ignorance of the true nature of marriage. Marry a friend and then work your whole life to build the friendship.

Partner

Marriage is a business decision. Many people live in denial of this reality, but it is true. Those who doubt the business side of marriage get a rude awakening if the marriage fails and they end up in divorce court. In ages past, marriage was often seen as nothing more than a business decision. Kings expanded their territory, made alliances, and played political games through marriage.

Marriage should never be only a business decision, but business must be seen as a component. While some couples work closely together and others completely separate work from home life, no one should foolishly ignore the fact that every spouse is a business partner—they influence your credit score, determine how you spend money, and own half of everything you own. One should never marry for business, but one should always keep business in mind. A good spouse is also a good business partner. They may not know the details of the business, but they know you well enough to point out blind spots and encourage strengths.

Lover

The major difference between friendship and marriage is the element of sexuality. While every marriage should include friendship, only one friendship should include sexual intimacy. That is marriage.

This aspect of marriage should neither be elevated as the most important part of marriage nor be diminished as a secondary role within the marital relationship. Sex is not the only thing, but it is important to the marital covenant. While most relationships start strong in the area of sexuality—it's often a driving factor for marriage—many couples falsely assume this aspect of marriage should develop naturally with little effort. It's a dangerous assumption. A strong sexual connection takes time, knowledge, wisdom, understanding, and a lot of trial and error.

Roommates, Girlfriend, or Pretty Woman

When one of the three elements is completely absent, the marriage digresses into a different type of relationship.

Where friendship and partnership are present but the spouses aren't lovers, they function like roommates. Having a roommate can make life better. Some of our closest relationships are formed in college when we have a partnership with some of our friends to share the costs of living expenses. But marriage is supposed to be more than a roommate relationship. The intimate connection between husband and wife is vital. It is uniquely distinguished from all others.

While this type of relationship can develop in any marriage, it is a real threat with adolescents in the house. Life can become chaotic, and the couple can lose their sexual connection so that they just operate as roommates. They communicate to keep the house running, but they have lost the intimate connection. Marriage is meant to be much more than the connection of two roommates.

Friends and lovers who are not partners fail to mature. They are still living as though they are dating. Before engagement, a relationship should grow in steps. Friendship should develop and begin to introduce aspects of intimacy (although I would encourage far less intimacy than most). As the couple decides they want to commit to each other, the engagement is a proclamation that they will become partners.

However, when they become partners only in theory and not in practice, they continue to operate as a dating couple. They might feel a close connection, but there is still distance between them. They might love each other, but they can't be certain the other person has their back. Marriage is meant to be much more than a boyfriend/girlfriend relationship.

Partners and lovers who do not have a good friendship have taken the beauty of marriage and exchanged it for a business transaction. Without friendship, marriage becomes something akin to prostitution. Everything is done for selfish reasons, where I do something for you so you will do something for me. Friends sacrifice for one another without any expectation of something in return. Without friendship, a husband and wife selfishly take care of themselves without thought of the other.

Where partnership and sex exist without friendship, trust is absent. Needs might be taken care of, but both parties will run the risk of feeling alone. Friendship can't be negotiated. Marriage is supposed to guarantee we always have someone by our side.

In a healthy marriage, both spouses play all three roles—friends, partners, and lovers. When we do, we give our spouse a precious gift: As friends we ensure someone is always on their side. As partners we guarantee someone always has their back. As lovers we let them know someone will always see their soul.

Marriage Works and the Works of Marriage

Marriage still works. We don't live in such a unique day that the vital institution that has been the bedrock of society since our beginning is suddenly an out-of-date relic. The value of a meaningful relationship is just as important today as in any time in the past. It might even be more important.

In a day when relationships are more surface than substance, a meaningful marriage can have even more benefit to a committed couple. On a regular basis I see it.

As I walk beside families in the best of times and the most challenging of circumstances, I see the difference between a strong marriage and one that struggles. The difference may be hidden from the public, but it is very prevalent to anyone who gets a peek into the inner circle.

Love matters.

> *As friends we ensure someone is always on their side.*
> *As partners we guarantee someone always has their back.*
> *As lovers we let them know someone will always see their soul.*

It's often most apparent in the effects it has on children. A child who grows up with parents who are unquestionably committed to each other is almost always radically different than one who is raised in a climate of uncertainty. As I speak with young couples considering marriage and talk through their issues, I rarely have to ask if their parents are still together. I know by the answers they give and the fears they have.

Communities, companies, and any collection of people greatly benefit when two people love each other with a consistent, life-giving love.

Marriage still works, but only if a couple is willing to do the works of marriage. It is not a passive relationship. A person needs to fully engage in order to reap the greatest benefits from marriage.

Some dramatically say, "Marriage is the hardest thing I've ever done." If that's true, then they have probably not done very many hard things.

But the statement is probably meant to combat the misconception that a good marriage just happens. It doesn't. Wherever you see a happy, healthy marriage, two people have made the effort to love, forgive, learn, and grow. Doing the work of marriage does not guarantee a good relationship, but refusing to do the work does guarantee a second-rate marriage at best, and more likely a marriage that is not able to sustain itself through the demands of life.

This book is about the practical side of making marriage work. In its simplest form, marriage is dependent on a couple developing three aspects of their relationship. While never being complete in any of the three, a healthy couple continually invests in each of these areas to be the spouses they need to be so they can have the marriage they desire.

BE INTENTIONAL

1. Do you believe staying in love is something more mysterious or more predictable? Why?

2. What do you think the average newlywed believes is the role of a spouse? How do those expectations differ from friend, partner, and lover?

3. Of the three roles, which do you need to work on? Which does your spouse need to improve?

4. Do you believe you can have a successful marriage? What does that look like to you?

PART 1

FRIEND

3

No Wonder You Don't Love Each Other

It's my way of attaining father-of-the-year status. Whenever I need to recover the affection of my children (or simply give my wife thirty minutes to herself), I take the kids to McDonald's. On one trip, after opening the milk and apples and ensuring everyone had the proper amount of ketchup, I noticed an elderly couple sitting next to the window. On their table sat two cups of coffee and a half-eaten cookie. Sitting across from one another, they were reading the newspaper.

I watched as they danced. They would read in silence for a bit, and then he would lower his paper and tell her about a news story. She would lower her paper to listen. They would converse for a moment, then both papers would be raised back to reading level. After a few minutes she would lower her paper and tell him about something in her section. He would lower his paper, they would converse about it, and then both papers returned to eye level.

This went on for the entire twenty minutes it took for my kids to eat. I don't know how long the couple had been there before us or how long they stayed there after us. But for twenty minutes I saw a perfect illustration of friendship in marriage.

When I pronounce two people husband and wife and send them back down the aisle hand in hand, they will often walk for a bit and then turn to one another, make eye contact, smile, and turn back ahead. When I see this I often think, *Keep doing that and you will be just fine.*

Marriage does not strip us of our individuality. We remain ourselves even as we bind ourselves into a committed relationship. We will keep living our individual lives even as we live together. Friendship is established as we weave our lives together with our spouse. Hand in hand we walk through life together, looking at what lies ahead, but regularly we look at one another, share a moment, and then turn back ahead.

Successful couples are continually looking ahead and then at each other, then back ahead and back at each other. It is a continual dance that empowers each spouse to live their individual lives but also helps them know they are fully loved, supported, and not alone.

Friendship is built on shared attention.

Friendship is built on shared attention. Two people make a connection often through a third element. For the couple in McDonald's it was a newspaper. They each engaged individually with the paper, but they would regularly turn to one another and have a shared experience. Every time they connected, their relationship was strengthened.

Good Is Better Together

At its best, marriage brings a tremendous gift—it makes good things better.

Good isn't fully good unless it is shared. Whenever we experience something good in life, we must share it with others. The sharing of the good multiplies the experience of it. Finding out you're going to have a grandchild is exciting, but sharing the news with everyone is far more fun. Hitting a hole in one is great, but retelling the story to every golfer or non-golfer you know is better. Eating a tremendous meal is wonderful, but telling your dinner party about the entrée or sharing your story with others is a vital part of the experience.

Good is meant to be shared. While it can be appreciated on an individual level, it finds most of its meaning in the midst of relationship with others.

Marriage ensures you always have someone with whom you can share the good. It attaches you to someone so that as you live your individual life, you can turn to them and share your experience. A beautiful sunset, a cute child, an interesting fact, a deep thought—anything that causes good feelings gives us a compulsion to share that experience with another person.

This desire helps nourish a marriage. It gives ample opportunity for us to have a positive experience with our spouse. Consider the reciprocal relationship—marriage gives us what we need by supplying someone with whom we can share the good, and we give marriage what it needs when we have a positive shared experience with that person.

While this process is not everything in marriage, it might be the most important aspect. Positive experiences build our friendship, and friendship is the foundation of marriage.

At its heart, marriage is meant to be a friendship. It's why I laugh when college students tell me they don't want to "risk the friendship" by asking out their best friend. I respond, "Tell the truth—either you are a coward or you don't think he/she is attractive. It has nothing to do with 'risking the friendship.'"

When two people go on a date, the most pressing question is, *Can I be friends with this person?* Yes, attractiveness matters. Yes, it is nice when there is a spark. But the main focus on the first few dates is whether or not this person is enjoyable to be around.

What begins as friendship should also continue as friendship. For the average couple, the most productive way they can improve their marriage is by intentionally focusing on deepening their friendship. When this occurs, partnership is easier and the sexual connection is often enhanced.

Friendship is about more than just positive experiences, but without positive experiences a friendship ceases. Many unhealthy marriages are out of balance because they are starving from a lack of positive interactions. These couples have failed to nourish the friendship spectrum, and their relationship has atrophied amid only negative interactions. This absence of good happens primarily in two ways.

First, some share with others what should be first shared with their spouse. They exchange their husband or wife for another person. Consider this: who would be the first person you would tell if your boss promoted you or you received exciting news or something you hoped would happen actually did take place?

If your spouse isn't consistently your first person, something is wrong with your relationship. They don't have to be your first person every time. Maybe they are busy, or maybe you have a friend who understands the good shot or good bargain better than your spouse. But in most situations, if your spouse is not the first person with whom you share good news, then they are not your best friend. And if this is the case, the relationship is not as healthy as it could be.

Aim to have your spouse be your first person. When we turn toward others before our spouse, we are robbing our relationship of the necessary positive interactions a healthy marriage requires. We are investing in other friendships at the expense of our spouse.

Notice I'm not insisting that you simply make sure you tell your spouse; I'm insisting that you tell them most things first. Before your friend, co-worker, parent, or child, make every effort to share good news with your spouse.

The first telling is rife with emotions and excitement that begin to fade with each additional telling. If I tell a story to my friend first and then to my wife, my wife will get less of me in the telling. She might get the facts, but she will not get my emotions. My wife deserves me more than my friends do, so she deserves to be my first person.

This isn't always possible. Yet as often as I can, I discipline myself to call my wife before anyone else regarding good news. By doing so, I'm investing in my marriage and enjoying the good.

Second, some couples miss the good because they overlook the importance of seemingly small moments. When we share the good, we aren't just sharing the moment; we're also sharing ourselves. Sadly, many couples only hear what is being offered on the surface and do not realize the deeper meaning. When your wife tells you about her day, she isn't just reviewing the facts of the day; she is revealing her heart. When your husband rewinds the game and asks you to watch a play, he isn't just inviting you to see the game; he's inviting you to see his soul. When your wife reads you a quote from a book, she is not telling you about the book; she is telling you about herself.

When we hear only the surface issue and not the deeper invitation, we miss the connection. What I'm doing in the moment—working, watching TV, reading a book, playing with the children—sometimes feels more important than the surface issue my wife mentions. But it is *always* less important than her.

When I hear her words as an invitation into her life more than as a specific issue, I will choose to listen. Listening will create a positive experience in which she feels heard, understood, respected, and valued.

Failing to respond in a positive way—by acting too busy, feigning interest, or rejecting the interaction—will make her feel rejected, unimportant, unknown, and unheard. Enough of these experiences train a spouse to find an outlet other than their husband or wife to share the good moments with.

Creating positive interactions with our spouse is necessary because the negative interactions within a marriage are guaranteed.

Feelings will be hurt. Miscommunication will occur. Misunderstandings will happen. Frustration, confusion, and conflict are an unavoidable aspect of even a healthy marriage.

Because these negative interactions will occur, it is vital that we provide our relationships with positive interactions. By doing so, the negative moments will be seen in their proper context. One negative interaction in a day of multiple positive interactions simply feels like part of life. However, one negative interaction in a day of only one interaction feels like an insurmountable obstacle in a relationship. If 100 percent of your interactions for a day are negative (not because you have multiple negative moments but because you have only very few moments), then your relationship can feel broken.

Healthy marriages do not have less conflict; they have more positive interactions.

Healthy marriages do not have less conflict; they have more positive interactions. The negative moments are minimized by the amount of positive emotions and feelings from the good moments. To give good moments to friends before we give them to our spouse is to starve our marriage of the very thing it needs to thrive.

Time Is a Prerequisite for Friendship

A friend asked me to lunch. After small talk we got to the real issue—his marriage was in trouble. He was frustrated, hurt, and confused. Things had been going so well. He had always loved his wife. His kids were great. Business had never been better. But for some reason his relationship with his wife had grown tense. There wasn't any specific issue. It just wasn't fun, and he felt as though they really didn't love each other anymore.

He expected me to be shocked. I wasn't. I have this conversation at least twice a week. So I asked a simple question: "How much time will you spend with your spouse today?" He stared at me, so I added, "An hour? Thirty minutes? Five minutes?"

As he began to recount the schedule of kids' ball games and school expectations, I rephrased the question. "How much quality, one-on-one time will you spend with your wife that does not revolve around the kids, work, or managing day-to-day life?" He laughed at the thought. Then I said what I was thinking. "Well, no wonder you don't love each other anymore."

What gives us the assumption that our feelings of love will continue for one another when we fail to do anything to actively invest in those feelings?

We all have friends we haven't seen in years, and we still feel the same way about them that we always have, but we notice one key thing about those friendships: while we haven't had the opportunity to deposit good moments into our relational bank, there also have not been any withdrawals. Since we haven't seen those friends, that means they haven't needed anything from us or needed us to serve them.

This is never true of family, particularly spouses. When a lengthy period of time passes without positive interactions with each other, our emotional balance is quickly depleted because we continue to make withdrawals on the relationship. We need help to keep life going. We have expectations of one another. Because we live with the person, they continue to see us at our worst.

It is not unusual for me to interact with couples who might physically be in the presence of one another, but emotionally, spiritually, and relationally, they haven't seen each other in months and sometimes years. By the time they call me, they are shocked their relationship has deteriorated. Meanwhile, I'm shocked they still have a relationship. Without any positive interactions, I'm amazed they are even in the same room.

Marriage requires friendship, and friendship requires time. This doesn't mean a couple has to spend hours together every single day. That would be impossible. Especially if kids are at home and both spouses are working, the demands of life will make spending time together very difficult. But a couple must find some time. They have to steal moments, even seconds, in which they can reconnect so they can endure the stresses of life.

Marriage requires friendship, and friendship requires time.

Beyond the stolen moments of a random day, couples must prioritize concentrated time together, knowing that it will come at the expense of something—work, time with the kids, etc. Without meaningful time together, a couple will at minimum forget whether they love one another and at maximum actually stop loving one another.

Love requires time. To the extent we choose to spend time with our spouse, we will likely feel love for them.

A Friendship Test

A simple test to diagnose the state of your friendship is to listen. What does your marriage sound like? Do you know what a dying marriage sounds like? Would you recognize it if you heard it?

We assume a bad marriage sounds like World War III, a catfight, or a heated debate between two political opponents. Yet most bad marriages sound the same. They sound silent. There is no arguing. No fighting. No discussion. Just silence. Silence before work. Silence after work. Silence while cooking. Silence while eating. Silence while watching TV. Silence while going to bed.

Then suddenly the silence is broken with laughter, conversation, and joy. What breaks the silence? Someone else. A friend calls, a child drops by, a co-worker comes for dinner. When someone else is in the house, it is full of joy, but when they leave, the silence returns.

You see your spouse engage a co-worker and you wonder, *Why won't he talk to me that way?*

You see her laugh with a child and you remember, *She used to laugh with me like that.*

You see him comfort a hurting friend and you think, *He has such compassion for others, but not me.*

What you don't realize is your spouse feels the same things about you. Notice how you talk to your child, friend, co-worker, pastor, bank teller, and even strangers compared to how you talk to your spouse. If you engage others more than your spouse, you are headed in the wrong direction.

Silent marriages have dangerous consequences:

Issues stay unresolved.

Hearts remain hidden.

Vulnerability is always rejected.

Depth is never experienced.

A marriage with lots of fighting can often end with one dramatic joust, but a silent marriage ends with a thousand words unsaid and neither spouse knowing where or when it went wrong.

Silence is a symptom of apathy. There is no use trying. No one is willing to take the risk and actually try to communicate. We've been rejected too many times. We have failed too often. So we no longer try. We tell ourselves to stop caring as a way to prevent hurt.

Yet there is another way. It's not the way of aggression. Don't start yelling to break the silence.

Many silent marriages have moments of yelling. One spouse is tired of the silence and tries to break it, yet the other spouse feels overwhelmed and one or both of them begin to shout. The message is heard loud and clear—don't break the silence or you will get violence.

The end to apathy is not aggression; it's meekness. It's the middle ground between aggression and apathy. It's attacking a problem, but never a person. It's communicating about difficult topics, but with humility. It's submitting every issue to a higher purpose and never blowing things out of proportion. It's understanding what matters and refusing to stay silent about it.

Meekness communicates that one spouse still cares about the marriage. It announces, "I'm still here." It shows concern for the other person. It reveals a vulnerability and welcomes the other person to reciprocate. Meekness reins in the aggressive and provokes the apathetic.

For some, meekness would say, "Stop yelling." For many, meekness would say, "Start talking."

Wonder if you operate with meekness? Consider the following questions:

Do you regularly resolve issues?
. Do you communicate your full heart to your spouse?
Are you able to talk about every issue without great fear? Money? Sex? In-laws?
Do you and your spouse protect each other's hearts?

If the answer to these questions is yes, you probably are operating with meekness. If the answer is no, consider what meekness would look like in response to each issue.

Silence is an often overlooked indicator of a bad marriage. Listen to your marriage. If it is yelling, your friendship is probably lacking. Yet if it is sadly quiet, your friendship is just as absent.

Friends talk. They communicate. They interact with one another. Your friendship with your spouse doesn't have to be your loudest relationship, but it must be a relationship filled with conversation. Without communication, you cannot be friends.

The By-product of Friendship

Time and conversation are natural elements that lead to friendship. A friendship might be able to endure a short season without them, but for the long haul the two are necessary to establish the type of lasting friendship a marriage requires.

Friendship results in something few people consciously realize but, when called to our attention, everyone recognizes as true. Friends are comfortable with one another.

Some might consider comfort the opposite of romance, but while comfort may not sound sexy, it is extremely appealing. Consider the pleasure of slipping into a comfortable sweatshirt and relaxing pants after a long day of work in the winter. Who doesn't daydream on occasion of that perfect beach location with a cool breeze and no obligations? The promise of comfort is a powerful draw for us.

We spend plenty of time uncomfortable. We have to impress some people, appease others, and speak carefully so we don't offend many. We live in a constant power structure where some have power over us and we have power over others. Our lives are in a continual state of tension.

It's the same word that describes many marriages—tense. I often hear phrases like, "I have to walk on eggshells" or "I just try not to rock the boat." These are signs the friendship between a couple is not where it needs to be. When married couples are also best friends, one overwhelming quality grips them—they are comfortable with one another.

This doesn't mean they completely let their guard down so that anything goes. We all need a filter and some restraint. But it does mean when the tension of life is too much, a healthy couple finds relaxation with one another. They enjoy spending time together because they don't have to put on a front. Their relationship, while never perfect, is a place in which they can find rest and rejuvenation.

Comfort connotes the concept of strength. Just as a fort is a stronghold for an army, the feeling of comfort is a relaxing state resulting from the confidence of strength. A healthy marriage makes us stronger. Emotionally, mentally, physically, we are stronger together than we are separated.

What I desire for my marriage is for it to be a fort—a safe place where Jenny and I can always find safety and comfort. Life can be difficult. We can feel at times as though we are under attack by many different elements, but it doesn't have to be that way at home. If we establish a deep friendship built on trust, deepened by quality time spent together and meaningful conversation, we can discover a level of comfort with one another that is unlike anything else. We can create a fort to protect us in difficult times.

A healthy marriage is defined as two great friends who are extremely comfortable with one another, living life together.

BE INTENTIONAL

1. Which way are you most tempted to steal the good from your marriage—by sharing with someone other than your spouse or by overlooking the good?
2. What have been some of your favorite moments in marriage? How can you create more like them?
3. Are you spending adequate time together for your friendship to develop? If not, how will you fix this?
4. How can you develop further comfort with your spouse?

4

The Most Overlooked Characteristic of Marriage

Standing ovations are rare occurrences at funerals, but this one seemed to fit the occasion. Her long struggle with cancer had ended three days earlier. It had been five years since I sat with the family and the doctor revealed the rare cancer diagnosis. Stunned, someone finally asked, "How long does she have?"

The doctor hesitated to answer. "It could be a few months or a few years. Absolutely best-case scenario with the most aggressive form of treatment and everything going her way . . . I'd say five years."

His educated guess was frighteningly accurate. Just past the fifth anniversary of her diagnosis, she made the decision to bring in hospice care and start the journey toward what comes next. But it wasn't an easy transition. The will that had allowed her to fight for so long was not easily dismissed. She lingered in great pain and exhaustion. One week gave way to another and then another. A month passed and then two and then three. On multiple occasions the family gathered at her side for the end, but the end did not come.

Finally, mercifully for her sake and the sake of the family, she breathed her last. And as he had been through it all, her husband was right by her side. As friends and family gathered three days later to pay their last respects, it seemed natural to take just a moment to recognize his service to his wife and his family over five years of painful treatments, setbacks, long road trips to the Mayo Clinic, and all the small acts that few people ever saw as he served her. So in his honor, we stood and applauded.

This man's gift to his wife is not as common as we might think. I've been fortunate to see it on many occasions, but there have been times in which I've seen the opposite response to sickness. More spouses run than we would like to admit.

Ashley's diagnosis wasn't life threatening, but it was serious. It was going to be a lengthy process through multiple surgeries, radiation, and possibly chemo to make sure her breast cancer did not take her life. Thankfully the diagnosis came early and the cancer was one of the easier types to treat. The road would be difficult, but if everything went well it would only be difficult for a few years before she returned full force to the life she wanted.

Unfortunately, David had very little interest in assisting her. I can only assume the marriage was in trouble long before the diagnosis was given, but when it came, David ran. Not in denial, or for a day or a week, but for good. He divorced her without even a hesitation. Ashley was alone during the surgery. By herself during the radiation. Thankfully chemo wasn't needed. She made it, but her cancer was a double sorrow because not only did she have to suffer, but she had to do so alone.

In my view, David's actions are the definition of cowardice. In the very moment he had the opportunity to step up and live out the vows he had spoken, he ran. In so doing, he robbed Ashley of what is supposed to be one of the great gifts of marriage—always having someone by your side.

At its heart, marriage is a friendship in which two people join hands and walk through life side by side. No matter what they might face, they face it together. The unknown aspect of life is what makes marriage so risky and what makes the vow to love so beautiful. We do not reconsider our love with every season of life. Instead, we vow to one another our very best no matter what might come—for richer or poorer, in sickness and in health.

In Sickness and in Health

"In sickness and in health." On two occasions I have said those words with full confidence that the couple repeating them actually knew what they meant. The first occurrence brought a smile to my face. She had endured, and marriage was her reward on the other side of illness. Together they had journeyed through the struggles of a serious disease as boyfriend and girlfriend. Now they would be husband and wife. They knew what "in sickness and in health" meant.

The second occurrence brought a tear to my eye. She had weeks to live. The vow renewal was his gift to her. I almost cut the words, fearing they might be too painful. But with a crowd gathered, I included them as a testimony to all who would hear them say, "In sickness and in health." They meant it and everyone knew it.

> *The unknown aspect of life is what makes marriage so risky and what makes the vow to love so beautiful.*

Few of us consider sickness and suffering when picking a mate. We consider how the other person might look in the morning or what bad habits they might have. We consider what offspring they could produce or what extended family they might bring to the reunion.

Yet few of us ever consider a vital question: "Can I suffer with this person?" It sounds like the beginning of a marriage joke, but it's not. It's a real question and one that should be explored by every dating couple. Suffering is a part of life. The older a person gets, the more we realize that suffering is not a rare occurrence but a common aspect of our lives. Sorrow comes in many forms, yet it is guaranteed to come.

Not everyone suffers well. Some live in denial, unable to confront the deep realities of life. Some live in despair, unable to recognize the convergence of laughter and tears. Few have the grace to suffer well. Those who do are a wellspring of life and faith.

Who do you want holding your hand when the test says cancer? On whose shoulder do you want to lean when the doctor says, "We've done all we can"? Who do you want to lie beside when you don't know where your child is or if they will ever come home? In whose eyes do you want to look when your world turns upside down? Find someone who suffers well.

I know it doesn't seem important when life is perfect. A beautiful smile is far more attractive than quiet determination. A common interest is far more appealing than internal strength.

Yet when life falls apart, you want someone you can run to, not someone you want to run from. You want someone who believes in you, who instills faith rather than doubt. You want someone who hopes no matter the circumstances.

Life is hard enough; there is no need to make it harder. Friends can't make life easy—no one can do that—but they do make it easier. They help carry the burden. They ease the pain. They lessen the load. When spouses are friends, life is sweeter. It is easier to suffer together than alone. Yet when a spouse fails to play the role of friend, every grief is stronger, every sorrow is more painful, and every hurt cuts deeper.

Spouses take the role of friend seriously when they

know how to suffer,

don't live in denial but confront the sorrows of life,

don't live in despair but know how to laugh and cry at the same time, offer support and hope in all of life's challenges, and see the big picture of life.

And then,

every grief is wedded with hope,
every sorrow is matched with love, and
every hurt is paired with healing.

One of the great guarantees of life is that every person, every couple, will suffer. When you do, you want someone by your side.

Trust Changes Everything

Suffering brings to light the key aspect of friendship—trust. We are friends with others to the extent that we can trust them. Where trust is absent, so is true friendship.

For a few years I had a minor skin tag just under one of my eyes. It didn't have any negative influence on my vision, but it was irritating. On a weekly basis, someone would stop me mid-conversation and say, "You have something under your eye." I would thank them but then let them know it wasn't anything I could just wipe away. It was a small growth I couldn't remove.

One day I asked my doctor, "Do you think you can do anything about this?" He looked at my eye and said, "I can try." He told me to drop by one day and he would try to remove it. So the next time I was near his office I dropped in. The process was fairly simple: lie down, close my eyes, and let a doctor use a sharp object to cut out a collection of cells underneath my skin. As I lay there, one thing struck me—how calm I was despite what was happening.

Obviously this wasn't major surgery, so there was no need for me to be really nervous, but there was a knife very near my eye. And still I was calm. Why? Because I trusted the doctor. I've known him for a long time. I knew he would never do anything to unnecessarily hurt me. I knew he wouldn't risk my eyesight for a skin tag. I knew if he was uncomfortable about any part of the process, he would stop and either tell me to live with the blemish or refer me to someone who could do the job.

Because I trusted him, I could relax and let him do his job. Even when it hurt, I could communicate the pain but accept it. I never doubted his ability. I never questioned what was happening. My trust in him allowed me to endure the process with a general sense of ease.

Trust changes everything. It even changes how I approach pain. Pain often reveals the level of our trust. Take me to a doctor I do not know and if I feel pain, I begin to question either his heart or his ability. Does he know what he's doing? Am I being seen by a hack? Does he care that he is hurting me? Yet when I know and trust my doctor, he can use sharp objects near my eye and it is not frightening. He can say, "This is going to hurt," and I know the pain is necessary and useful. I can endure the pain because I trust the person.

So it is in marriage. *Painless* has never been used to describe a healthy marriage. While marriage should be a positive experience most of the time, there are moments in marriage that are supposed to be extremely difficult. As our weaknesses and inadequacies are revealed, the revelation process is painful. When trust isn't present within the marriage, the pain is almost unbearable. However, when trust is present, a couple can confront and endure nearly anything. And endure is what every couple has to do.

> **Painless** *has never been used to describe a healthy marriage.*

You are not the perfect couple. No couple is. No matter how good a marriage may look on the outside, no matter how much you might envy the husband or wife, every relationship has setbacks, struggles, and moments of great trouble. Some deceive themselves into thinking their marriage is perfect, while far more attempt to deceive others that their marriage is perfect. It's all a lie. Yet that perception some try to portray strangles a marriage. It prevents a couple from getting the help they need. They can never attend a marriage conference for fear that people might talk. They can never go to marriage counseling for fear that someone might see their car in the parking lot. They can never ask for help lest they sacrifice the mirage that they have it all together.

But no one has it all together. Until a couple is willing to admit that they are not the perfect couple, they have very little chance of having a meaningful, healthy relationship. Yet there is nothing more liberating than being willing to embrace your imperfections. It keeps you from feeling the pressure to put on a good front for others. It allows you to expect struggles and mistakes. It empowers you to get the help necessary whenever you confront a problem you can't solve on your own.

Love and Ignorance

Whenever I'm performing a wedding ceremony, particularly for a young couple, I begin the formal address by saying, "There are two things I can guarantee you. One, you are clearly in love with one another. Two, you have no idea what you are doing." The second line always gets a great laugh from the married couples in the room—because it is unexpected but also true.

Ignorance should be one of the great joys of a new marriage. A man and a woman step into marriage with very little understanding of what makes it work. And that is okay. It's supposed to be that way. One of the fun aspects of marriage should be two people who don't know what they are doing learning and growing together. No pretending. No posturing. No assumptions that they have it all figured out.

While we learn a lot in marriage, especially early in the marriage, that basic ignorance doesn't necessarily leave. While I'm confident with what it takes to be married for a decade or two, I have no idea what will be demanded of us in the third, fourth, and maybe fifth decades. I know where we have been and what we have learned, but I do not know everything we need for the next season of life. Those are the things we will have to learn together.

Marriage should begin (and continue) with a deep humility born from an understanding that you've never been here before, but you are excited to be ignorant together. You are excited to learn, struggle, and figure out how to have a good marriage. This humility causes a couple to expect problems, mistakes, and misunderstandings. It will allow them to more easily laugh when things do not go as expected or to put a fight in the proper context, knowing the marriage isn't over because of one disagreement.

When couples assume they know what they are doing, they run a great risk of allowing their ignorance to be their undoing. They will close their ears to the advice of others and close their minds to any thought beyond what they already believe. Having seen their parents' marriage, having watched marriage displayed on television, and having had their own relationships, these couples arrogantly enter into marriage assuming they know everything they need to know about the relationship. Nothing could be further from the truth.

How can a person know about marriage if they have never been married? How can a person know about being married to this person even if they have already been married to someone else? How can they be certain about what will be required of them next year when they have never lived it? It's impossible. Yet every year I perform ten to fifteen wedding ceremonies for couples who assume they know (or pretend to know) everything about what to expect. Stop assuming. Stop pretending. Marriage should not be entered into arrogantly, but humbly. And it should continue to exist in a climate of humility.

Humility is what allows us to trust one another. We can trust humble people because we know they will not overstep their ability.

They will recognize their faults and inadequacies. They will not try to put on a front. They will not think of themselves as more valuable than others. Humble people are trustworthy people.

Those filled with pride are the ones we cannot trust. They will lie, cheat, manipulate, and deceive. They will see themselves as above the rules or beyond the need to explain themselves. Any action will be justifiable in their eyes if it helps them attain their desires.

Pride is the ultimate enemy of marriage. It decays a marriage from the inside out. Where pride is present, intimacy is absent because a prideful person cannot be trusted or respected. They can only be feared, questioned, and doubted.

Marriages flourish in humility. In the absence of self-righteousness, self-sufficiency, and self-reliance, marriages have the ability to thrive. In the presence of all the "selfs," nothing but selfishness can grow. Pride destroys trust because trust is built on the conviction that the other person will watch out for our best interests. Pride demands that only the interests of its occupant can have priority.

Pride kills friendship because pride can only befriend itself. It doesn't have the capacity to care for another or to submit its own desires to that of another.

My favorite definition of pride is "self-intoxication." In the same way that too much alcohol can inebriate us, pride has the ability to cloud our judgment. When a police officer wants to see if a driver is intoxicated, he asks the person to complete a few tasks—walk a straight line, say the ABCs, or touch their nose. These are simple tasks for those who are not drunk, but they are nearly impossible for those who are intoxicated. Being drunk makes a simple task difficult.

The same is true in marriage. When a husband or wife is self-intoxicated, easy tasks become difficult. Is it hard to serve your spouse? Do you struggle with submitting your desires to that which is best for your marriage? Is forgiveness a tough subject between the two of you? In a marriage built on humility, a husband or wife finds it generally easy to love, serve, forgive, and place themselves behind the well-being of the couple. When pride is present, these easy tasks become difficult. Trust erodes and the friendship is severed.

Whoever is humble is trustworthy; whoever is trustworthy is a friend. Friendship in marriage occurs within the climate of trust, which is established because of a shared humility between husband and wife. The absence of trust within a relationship does not always make itself apparent. It often stays hidden below the surface, affecting the relationship through other avenues. Many communication issues are trust issues. If a wife does not trust her husband, she cannot fully communicate her heart to him. If a husband does not trust his wife, he will continually hide his heart out of fear.

Many sexual disagreements arise from an absence of trust. Sex often touches on our deepest insecurities. It makes us vulnerable, and unless we can trust the person we are intimate with, we will be guarded. *Skittish* is the antithesis of *sexy*. If you trust your partner, you can openly communicate likes, dislikes, desires, and fears. Where trust is absent, few issues can be discussed and many assumptions are made.

> **Skittish** is the antithesis of **sexy**.

What many couples experience as a marital rut is actually occurrences of distrust. While every couple experiences seasons of what feels like being stuck, when a couple stays in a stagnant season for a long period of time, it is likely because of distrust. They are stuck because they have reached the boundaries of their trust. Unless they learn to trust more, they will never grow deeper as a couple.

Trust changes everything. It is a quality of marriage that must consistently be developed. Much like a muscle, trust can be strengthened or weakened.

Sadly, many couples know the pain of sexual or financial or emotional betrayal. Trust has been shattered and the relationship suffers because of it.

Thankfully, trust can be regained. Slowly, in a baby-step fashion, even the worst of betrayals can be overcome as a couple rebuilds their trust. It can't happen too quickly, or what will develop is a pseudo-trust, where one or both spouses pretends to trust but always suffers from great doubt. But if a couple does the work, admits the deception, seeks to rebuild the relationship, and time and time again proves themselves trustworthy, trust can be rebuilt.

From Altar to Altar

When I was a little boy, my paternal grandfather would stay with us when my grandmother was in the hospital. It only happened a few times, but those nights are cemented in my memory. My grandfather went to bed early—even before me, an eight-year-old. My room was the only one with an extra place to sleep, so my mom would pull out the trundle bed, and I would sleep on it while my grandfather slept on my bed.

I remember one night in particular in which my grandfather was staying with us and went to bed thirty minutes before me. At the right time, my parents told me it was bedtime, so off I went. But as I neared the room, I could hear my grandfather talking. I quietly peeked through the crack in the door and saw him kneeling beside the bed, praying. I probably shouldn't have stood there to listen, but I did. He was praying for the health of his wife, asking God to make her better. I left the doorway and told my parents why I couldn't go to bed yet. They told me to wait a few minutes and try again. I did and he was still praying. Finally, on the third try, his prayers were over and we could both go to sleep.

At the time I wasn't sure why, but I knew it made me feel good to hear my grandfather praying for my grandmother. While I felt bad for his pain, I was comforted by his love for her because I also knew he had a similar love for me.

All these years later, I look back on that night with a much deeper respect. I know many husbands pray for their wives, but not all do. I know many wives serve their husbands even in the most difficult of moments, but not all do. Anyone can kneel at the altar in a white dress or tuxedo and boldly proclaim their undying love and devotion to another person. It is something far different to actually live out that love and devotion over a lifetime of ups and downs.

Marriage might begin at the altar of a church, but it is proven at the self-made altar of a bedside at a hospital, a nursing home, or even your grandson's bedroom. A true friend is always on your side no matter what circumstances you may face. The privilege of marriage is to be the ultimate friend to our husband or wife through a variety of seasons.

"Can I suffer with this person?" is an important question. We will all suffer, and when we do, we deserve to have our husband or wife right beside us even in the midst of the pain. Trust is at the core of a good marriage. Show me a couple who trusts one another and I will show you a couple who can endure any circumstance. Without trust, intimacy dies. With trust, it flourishes.

BE INTENTIONAL

1. Do you know how to suffer well? How can you further develop your endurance so you can be a good spouse?
2. Does your spouse have legitimate reasons not to trust you in specific areas of your relationship? If so, how can you prove yourself trustworthy?
3. What makes you feel most supported by your spouse during the difficult moments of life?
4. In what ways has pride hurt your friendship with your spouse?

5

Give Thanks and Play

Traffic court seems like an odd place for a date, but when you're raising a couple of kids, each leading an organization, and just trying to stay afloat in the chaos of life, sometimes you take whatever you can get.

Jenny was in a minor traffic accident in our driveway. While many cars get hit in a driveway, it is highly unusual to be hit by a random stranger in your own driveway. But that is exactly what happened. I'm still not sure what the guy was thinking, but as Jenny started to pull into our narrow driveway on the right, the driver behind her tried to pass her on that side and ran right into her.

Despite his guilt, the driver was very kind. The police showed up and wrote him a ticket, and we thought the ordeal was over. But a few months later Jenny was subpoenaed to testify in traffic court. The driver thought he should not have received a ticket for hitting my wife in our driveway and was fighting the fine.

In my home state, traffic court is a nuisance for everyone. Primarily it is a bunch of guilty people trying to get out of a fine they could easily pay. Their refusal takes up the time of the court, police officers, and average citizens who need to be somewhere else. In order to combat the nuisance, traffic court is scheduled in the most inconvenient of ways. It is the last section of an afternoon session, normally beginning around 4:00 p.m. However, in order for your case to be heard at that time, you have to arrive before 1:00 for check-in. In the three hours following, the court hears a string of cases normally revolving around drugs, shoplifting, and other petty crimes.

While Jenny had nothing to worry about, she was a bit nervous about testifying in court, so she asked if I would go with her. For three hours we watched as others pleaded their cases. Strangely, it was one of the best dates we've had in years.

We had a great time. Rare is the case in which Jenny and I are seated that close together in a room full of people with no children and no cell phones. It felt as though we were high school sweethearts sitting in class, trying not to get in trouble with the teacher.

We were seated behind an elderly couple who were apparently present to show support to a grandchild who had a drug issue. For thirty cases in a row, the couple sat quietly as the judge listened to the charges and gave her ruling. Some went to prison, some to county jail, but most received some form of the following sentence: "That's X years probation, suspended, and $300 fine. See the bailiff." This refrain was broken when a woman pled guilty to shoplifting from Walmart. The judge gave her normal sentence— "X years probation, suspended, $300 fine"—but then added, "and a lifetime ban from all Walmarts."

Upon hearing that, the quiet grandmother in front of me gasped in horror. I nearly lost it. Send someone to prison and the grandmother nodded in agreement. Ban someone from shopping at Walmart and she acted like it was the end of the world.

I couldn't stop laughing. It became like a funeral laugh, where it really isn't that funny but the expectation of being quiet and somber made the laughter harder to control. Jenny was looking at me; everyone was looking at me. She kept shushing me, but I couldn't help myself.

Thankfully, the plea bargains ended and traffic court began. The driver who had hit Jenny apparently had watched too much *Law & Order*, because for twenty minutes he attempted to pull every TV lawyer stunt possible. The judge patiently allowed him to put on his show, and when it was all over she asked one simple question: "Sir, were you driving behind Mrs. Thompson on the date in question, and did you hit her car?" He began to answer, "Yes, but—" However, before he could get out a third word, the judge said, "Then you're guilty, pay your fine, and get out of here."

On our way home from court, Jenny and I talked about what a good time we had that afternoon, as strange as it sounds. Maybe we were so starved for any time together that even time in a courtroom was enjoyable. Maybe it was being in a strange setting that bonded us together. But more likely it was the fact that wherever we go, we attempt to have fun.

Friendship and fun go hand in hand. Having fun isn't necessarily the most important aspect about friendship, but it does play an important role in determining whether or not we become friends. Consider a small toddler and her mother playing peekaboo. The game has a deep purpose. They are building a bond. The lighthearted interaction creates a deep bond between mother and daughter.

Few things breed intimacy or reveal intimacy as much as playfulness. Friends have fun, and having fun creates friends.

Few things breed intimacy or reveal intimacy as much as playfulness. Friends have fun, and having fun creates friends. Think back to your first friendships. Chances are they were formed on the playground. As you age, the method for forming friends doesn't greatly change. Even as an adult, we tend to become friends with the parents of our children's teammates. We have fun as we watch our kids having fun.

If you didn't have fun with your spouse on your first few dates, I doubt there would have been very many more dates, much less a marriage.

Having fun is an important aspect of friendship, which means it should be an important aspect of marriage. When we lose our ability to have fun as a couple, the loss has dramatic consequences on the relationship.

How often do you laugh together as a couple? What amazes me about laughter is that it has very little to do with outward circumstances and everything to do with the people involved. Everyone knows someone who is funny no matter the situation. While we don't have to be clowns in order to be good spouses, we do need the ability to connect with our husband or wife in a humorous way.

Oftentimes bad circumstances can lead to just as much laughter as good situations. Enduring difficult times can forge a bond even stronger. Healthy people seek the humorous elements in even the most tragic of situations. I have laughed hysterically with families in the hospice wing at a hospital, even though every person in the room was heartbroken. If laughter is part of the DNA of a family, it doesn't stop even in hospice. It seems as though the healthiest of marriage partners cry easily and laugh easily.

Yet playfulness is hard to maintain in a marriage. Without intention, the fun can disappear as the demands of life become nearly overwhelming.

How Playfulness Is Lost

I assume most couples begin with playfulness in their relationship. Yet over time, different circumstances erode the fun away. Three common factors are distrust, weariness, and a marital rut.

Distrust

Nothing destroys playfulness as much as distrust. The centerpiece of playfulness is opening oneself up to another for interaction. If we do not trust one another, we cannot be truly playful with one another. The importance of trust is one reason that playfulness is more of a presenting characteristic than the actual issue at play. Its absence is a symptom of a much deeper disease.

Weariness

Playfulness has the appearance of uselessness. While it is vital to the relationship, engaging in playfulness can feel like a waste of time. If we are tired, we will not feel the freedom or have the energy and creativity necessary to be playful. Most couples I see remain playful in their marriage until they have their first child. When the weariness of pregnancy sets in, many lose their playfulness and are never able to regain it. A refusal to maintain margin in their private lives and an unwillingness to invest in rest eats away at a couple's ability to have fun.

A Marital Rut

The relationship between playfulness and creativity is such that being in a rut can hinder both. As we repeat the daily routines over and over, we lose our sense of wonder, excitement, and joy. Just as play is a natural aspect of a healthy child's day, so too is playfulness a natural characteristic of a healthy marriage. The presence of play is predictable, but the actual playfulness creates variety. When it's absent, the relationship becomes boring. I'm not sure if the absence of playfulness causes the rut or if the rut causes us to lose our playfulness, but the two definitely go hand in hand.

How Playfulness Is Regained

While distrust, weariness, and a marital rut can erode playfulness, we can also rediscover it. We can rebuild the habit into our relationships. Several characteristics determine the reestablishment of playfulness.

Restored Trust

This takes the most time, but true playfulness can't exist without it. A relationship is destined to die if it goes too long without trust. Thankfully, trust can be rebuilt. By consistently being truthful, faithful to your word, and loving, you can restore trust. Many times couples expect it to be rebuilt much faster than is realistic. I often tell people that they can't walk the wrong way for ten years, turn around, and then, after walking ten minutes, expect to be in the right place. Trust can be built back faster than it was destroyed, but it may take longer than we like.

Rest

If trust is present, rebuilding playfulness becomes easy. Often the simplest task is to rest. As difficult as it is, find ways to give the best of your day to a spouse. It clearly can't happen every day because of work, children, and the demands of life, but if your spouse gets time with you only at the end of the day when you are the most tired, it will be difficult to enjoy each other's company. On occasion, give your spouse your best. When you are most awake, most refreshed, most alive, give that time to the one you love the most.

Shared Experiences

Playfulness is often built off shared experiences. Inside jokes, stories only the two of you know, and being able to link a current situation to a past experience can be vital to being playful. By having shared hobbies, learning something new together, or making sure you spend regular time together, you can build opportunities for playfulness.

A Change of Scenery

If a marital rut can erode playfulness, a change of scenery can quickly inject it back into a relationship. Even a crowded courtroom with shoplifters can be enough of a change of pace to allow playfulness to come forward. If playfulness is missing in your relationship, consider this: when was the last time you took an extended trip with just your spouse? Sleep in, explore a new place, and watch how your conversation is different by being in a different place with different expectations and none of the demands of home.

Turn It Off; Turn It Back On

When the fun in a marriage is lost, sometimes the couple needs to start over. I wonder, when Bill Gates experiences problems with his computer, does he turn it off and turn it back on? I assume so. Even one of the greatest computer minds to ever exist probably has to occasionally do a hard reboot.

As it is with computers, so it is with marriage. Every marriage needs a reset button. No matter how good a marriage might be, every couple hits rough spots. We have moments, and sometimes months, that are difficult. The question is not whether a couple will have difficult times, but how they will handle the difficult times when they come.

One thing good couples learn in marriage is how to hit the reset button when tough times come. Good couples reset the marriage when they have bad moments; great couples hit the reset button even when times are not that bad.

I officiated at a wedding ceremony at the most beautiful location for weddings in the region where I live. It was atop a mountain at a state park. As the wedding came to an end, I paused. I turned my back to the crowd and stood beside the couple, encouraging the newlyweds to take in the view and the moment. I told them, "When tough times come (and they will), when doubts arise (and they will), and when you don't know if you want to keep going, find a mountain. Find a place that reminds you of this moment, of this feeling, and of these promises you have made to one another."

What I was telling the couple was that they would forever have a reset button in their marriage. Every time they climb a mountain, they can remember. They can put their current circumstances in the context of bigger issues and remember why they love one another.

We all need a reset button. We need a place, activity, or routine we can run to when our marriage experiences a rough moment or season.

Each couple must create their own reset button, but here are five possibilities.

Location

Maybe it's where you had your first date or where you went on your honeymoon. Maybe it's your favorite vacation spot or your back porch. Find a location where you can go so that as soon as you get there, your stress goes down and the positive feelings begin to recharge.

Activity

Every couple needs to have at least one activity they enjoy doing together. Whether it's playing tennis or going on a hike, find something you both enjoy that allows for an escape from the normal routine. For Jenny and me, few things help reset our marriage as much as a walk. It forces conversation and allows us to discuss things we otherwise wouldn't.

Friends

Some friends just make you feel better. As a couple, you should have friends who cause you to love one another more. Maybe their marriage is so great, it encourages you. Maybe they make you laugh so much, you forget your problems. Whatever it is, notice the people in your life who cause the love for your spouse to grow, and then make an effort to spend more time with those people.

Conferences and Retreats

Never underestimate the impact of a weekend spent focused on your marriage at a conference or retreat. It gives you the opportunity to learn new skills, be reminded of old truths, and spend time focused on one another.

Vacation

This is my favorite reset button. Anytime Jenny and I can get away from the routine of work and kids, our marriage grows closer. It's not a reset button we can hit every day, but it is an annual opportunity for us to grow closer together. If you do not get away with your spouse on at least a yearly basis, stop right now and plan a trip.

There are moments in which every couple needs to clear the slate, be reminded of what is important, and renew their love for one another. While marriage may not come with a built-in reset button, we can create habits that allow us to reunite, remember our love, and reengage life with an invigorated connection with one another.

Don't Confuse Having Fun with Making Fun

While playfulness and fun are vital to a healthy relationship, there is a counterfeit that masquerades as fun but destroys a relationship—making fun of one another.

Fun in a marriage should be a mutually beneficial interaction that encourages both partners and draws them closer together. However, many couples actually abuse and put down one another in the name of "fun," with damaging effects.

Eric was a gifted communicator. He could entertain crowds and move them to action with tremendous skill. But he had a bad habit. Whenever he was in front of a new audience, he would make fun of his wife. It was a nervous tendency he thought was meaningless. Yet anyone who watched his wife as he did this would see it wasn't meaningless. It was damaging.

What Eric also didn't realize was that his audience didn't really find the jokes funny. They laughed out of nervousness more than humor. Ask Eric and he would say, "I don't mean it." But he clearly does. He would say, "She doesn't care," but she clearly does. He would say, "They think it's funny," but they clearly don't.

Playfulness does not mean having fun at the expense of your spouse.

Playfulness does not mean having fun at the expense of your spouse. It means engaging them in fun. Even if your spouse can't cook, drive, or add, don't air those faults in public. While playfulness is a sign of a healthy marriage, being playful is different than being hateful.

Most spouses don't mean it that way. A majority of comments meant in jest are just poorly thought-through comments aiming for a cheap laugh. The intent is rarely evil, but the actions still need to stop. The reward is not worth the risk.

When I hear a man make fun of his spouse in public, I often wonder, *If he will say that about her in public, what will he say to her in private?* It's okay to laugh about a situation. It can be enjoyable to remember a funny story. But it is never right to get a cheap laugh at the expense of our spouse.

As someone who is on stage on a regular basis, I have two basic rules to make sure I'm not using my wife for a cheap laugh. First, I never tell a story in which the audience will take my side over hers. They always side with her. I'm always the ignorant one or the wrong one, and she is always the hero. Not every life event happens that way, but I will only publicly tell of the situations that fit that scenario. Second, if there is any question in my mind of how she might feel about a story, I ask her opinion first. If she doesn't like it, I don't tell it.

Couples must be open and honest with one another in this area, or they could hurt one another without realizing it. If your spouse tells a joke or story you don't like at a party, on the way home it is important to say, "I know you meant nothing by it, but that story embarrassed me," or "I would prefer if you don't tell that story again."

Gratitude

Playfulness is most often born from a sense of gratitude. The more grateful one feels for their spouse, the more playful they are and the more they seek to have fun. Marriage is best lived in gratitude.

When Jenny and I were first married, I was in graduate school in Alabama. A friend called me and invited me to play in a golf tournament in Philadelphia, but we wouldn't get back until the day of our anniversary. Having just gotten married, I never considered this might be an invitation I would want to turn down. So I asked Jenny if I could play, saying I would be back in time to take her to a celebratory dinner, and she agreed.

> *Playfulness is most often born from a sense of gratitude.*

I flew to Philadelphia, played golf for a couple of days, and headed home on our anniversary. The plan was for me to fly from Philly to Newark to Atlanta. I would then drive from Atlanta to Birmingham and would be home by midafternoon.

We got to Newark without any problem, but when we landed I noticed it was foggy. When I made it to my gate I found out my flight had been canceled. The ticket agent told me the bad news that because of weather only limited flights were getting out, and I would likely be stuck in Newark all night. I explained my situation and asked if I could fly standby. She pointed me to a wall and told me everyone there was trying to fly standby. She was kind but firm when she said, "Son, it looks like you're in trouble."

I didn't know what to do, so I just sat by the wall and waited. As the next flight loaded, not a single standby passenger got on.

Everything was booked. Just as they were closing the door to the jetway, a flight attendant came through the door and whispered to the ticket agent. The agent got on the microphone and said, "Will K. Thompson please come to the desk?"

I jumped up and ran to the desk. She said, "Are you K. Thompson?" When I said yes, she handed me a ticket and said, "Hurry up, you are on that flight." I ran down the jetway toward the plane.

As soon as I stepped on the plane, the flight attendant asked, "Are you Thompson?" When I said yes, she pointed me to the first row and said, "You are right here." The "right here" was in first class. I was shocked. I had never flown first class before.

The door was quickly shut, and the plane pushed back from the gate. Within minutes we were in the air.

First class was like a whole different world. They brought me cookies, magazines, and newspapers. The seats were large and there was plenty of room. I thought everything was amazing.

The man sitting next to me disagreed. He was having a horrible day. Dressed in a suit, drinking strong drinks, and huffing at anything that didn't go his way, he looked miserable. To make his day worse, the happiest man in the world was sitting next to him and was thrilled at everything.

Finally the man looked over and sarcastically said, "Is this your first time in first class?" I told him it was and then proceeded to tell him the story of how I got on the plane. "That doesn't sound right," he said. "Let me see your ticket." So he took my ticket and everything looked normal to him, but that's when I saw it. The name on the ticket was Keith Thompson.

I'm not sure what happened to Keith Thompson that foggy day in Newark, but Kevin Thompson made it to Atlanta and drove back to Alabama to take his wife to dinner on their anniversary. It was the best flight ever.

Isn't it amazing how two men can sit side by side on the same plane, both in first class, headed to the same place, and have such radically different experiences? One was thrilled at everything and the other was frustrated by everything. What was the difference?

Gratitude. I didn't deserve to be on the plane and I knew it. Everything was a blessing to me. The other man not only thought he deserved to be on the plane, but he was a little frustrated I got there in an undeserving way. Everything was horrible to him.

Marriage is far better lived in gratitude. Friendship is most meaningful when we are grateful to know the other person and to have the opportunity to love and be loved by them. It doesn't mean everything will be perfect. It doesn't mean every scenario will bring a smile to our face and a sense of peace to our heart. But it does mean even the bad times will be viewed within the context of a much larger and more important story. It means we won't overlook the smallest of successes or achievements. It will empower us to see the good in our spouse. It will give us a deep sense of appreciation for the opportunity to love another person and to receive their love.

Where gratitude is present, so is a great marriage. Where gratitude is present, a couple feels the freedom to laugh and play. They do not feel the need to put on a show. Though life still has its demands, the presence of gratitude helps a couple not be overwhelmed by them. Each person can take the time to look one another in the eye and feel appreciation for the opportunity to walk this life hand in hand.

BE INTENTIONAL

1. Describe a time you and your spouse turned a negative experience (like traffic court) into a fun time that helped your relationship.

2. Can your relationship be described as playful? If not, why not?

3. Does your marriage have a reset button? What time, place, or event can help you regain the sense of fun in your relationship?

4. What makes you feel a deep sense of gratitude for your spouse, your marriage, and your life?

6

My Best Friend, Not My Only Friend

Being a good spouse is demanding. It is not enough to play one role; we must play three. Unless we are a friend, partner, and lover, we are failing to give our spouse everything we have promised and everything they deserve.

One of the primary responsibilities of a couple is to continually develop and nourish a deep friendship in every stage of a relationship.

It begins with dating. This is one reason sex should be saved for marriage. When sex enters into a relationship too quickly, it stunts the growth of the friendship. At a time in which two people should be exploring the personalities of one another, sex clouds their thinking and hinders decision making.

It continues in the earliest aspects of marriage. As dating gives way to marriage and life is lived together, deep bonds should be formed. This early stage can be one of the toughest and most challenging times as a young couple realizes the complexities of living with another person. This is another reason sex should be saved for marriage. At the time in which early struggles present themselves (two people learning to live together), we have a great gift to keep us together (the awakening of sexual intimacy).

It solidifies while having children. At this point a true partnership should be formed as a couple attempts to juggle all the pressures of living and raising a family. This stage of life is much more difficult to navigate alone than together. By working together, a couple can thrive in the midst of a very exhausting period of life.

It fully blooms with an empty nest. If a couple does the work necessary to build a true friendship, its full effects are not experienced until later in life. Having grown through so many different seasons and experiences, a mature friendship becomes nearly immovable. While problems still arise, the couple is so experienced in dealing with conflict and so confident from past experiences that the problems do not create any fear. Both individuals find their greatest satisfaction in living life with one another.

Husbands and wives are meant to be best friends.

Marriage is meant to be a relationship between two best friends. Husbands and wives are meant to be best friends. My wife is my first person and forever should be. She's my best friend, but she isn't my only friend.

While some overlook the importance of building friendship within marriage, others misunderstand the role of a spouse. They believe their spouse should be their only friend. They expect their spouse to fill every relational need that arises. They assume one person can fill the role of eight to ten people. That concept is fraught with peril.

A spouse is supposed to be our best friend, but they are never expected to be our only friend. It is a role they should not play, cannot play, and hopefully do not want to play. We need other friendships. We need friends who enjoy activities our spouse does not. We need peers going through similar experiences who can lend a listening ear or offer support when we are in need. Everyone needs friends, and a spouse is not enough. Expecting our spouse to be our only friend (or expecting us to be their only friend) is demanding too much.

I want to be my wife's best friend, but I also want her to have other friends. There are things I don't want to talk about. There are things I don't want to do. There are things I don't want to care about. As long as she has another friend, she experiences the love and support she needs without me having to listen to, accompany, or care about every aspect of what is going on. I care about her, but I don't have to care about every shot she hit in the tennis match. I don't have to debate what ingredient is best in a recipe. I don't have to be the only person with whom she discusses whether she should fire an employee or get them extra training.

Obviously if she wants me to listen, accompany, or care, then I will—because I care about her. However, if some of those roles can be fulfilled by other people, we will both be better for it.

Every Couple Needs a Couple

You need somebody. And probably somebodies.

I was discouraged about a parenting issue. When talking with a friend, I brought up my disappointment. My friend, being a few steps further down the parenting road than me, told me a few stories. His experience mimicked mine, but the future I feared was different from his experience. He gave me hope.

We all need people like this in our lives. We need people who are one, two, or three steps further along in life and can speak truth to us about the future. This is especially true in marriage.

One of the great privileges of my life is having many deep relationships with people from every stage of life. I can't imagine doing life without them. Jenny and I regularly listen to and learn from those who have been through our current stage of marriage.

They can encourage us. Laugh with us. Laugh at us. And let us know we will make it too.

Without them, we wouldn't know if our problems were unique or common, if we were the only ones who weren't perfect, how we could navigate certain issues, or whether others cared about our marriage. Having relationships with people who are further down the road than you can provide a tremendous resource and encouragement for your marriage.

Without those people, we will be left to our peers or ourselves. While peers are necessary, they cannot give us what we need to better our marriage. Peers are meant to walk beside us through life. Our friendship with them is often established as we experience life together. But generally speaking they are no smarter than we are.

We need others who have had more experience, knowledge, and time dealing with the issues we face. We need people who have been there and done that as we begin to get there and start doing that. Having relationships with couples who have been married ten, twenty-five, or even fifty years longer provides a deep context for marriage.

When they say our problems are normal, we can believe them. When they encourage us to seek help, we can listen to them. When they tell us we will be just fine, we can believe them. They have credibility in what they say. They may not know it all, but they know more than we do.

While these relationships are a natural part of the pastorate, they often do not form naturally within our lives. To have them, we need to be intentional in creating them.

Church, social clubs, country clubs, family friends, and work provide opportunities to build relationships with other couples. While relationships are good, intentional friendships are better. Here's the amazing thing that too many people fail to realize: most healthy couples would love to assist another couple with their marriage. If asked, they will help.

Every couple needs to find one or two other couples whose marriage they admire and intentionally become their friends. Tell them what you want. Let them know you admire their relationship and you want to spend time with them to learn. Have dinner, go to events, and find time to interact with them. In doing so, you will see them interact with each other, learn from their experience, and find ways to improve your own marriage.

Every couple needs to find one or two other couples whose marriage they admire and intentionally become their friends.

They will not be perfect. You will not want to copy everything you see. But even their flaws can be helpful to your marriage as you realize no one is perfect.

They can help you and you will help them. Every older couple is helped as they interact with younger couples. It will remind them of the importance of being role models, which will encourage them to make wise choices. Interacting with younger couples can also reinvigorate a seasoned marriage, reminding the older couple of the passion and excitement they might have once felt.

Cross-generational relationships can assist both the young and the old. Every couple needs another couple they can learn from and encourage.

Marriage Changes Friendships

While we need many more friendships than just the one with our spouse, vowing our life to another person should radically transform every other relationship. In part, it changes how we relate to friends of the same sex. While these relationships are vital, they must submit to our primary relationship with our spouse. I've seen many marriages destroyed just as they are beginning because one or both spouses are in denial about their new responsibilities as a husband or wife.

In many of these occasions, one spouse is refusing to make their husband or wife their best friend. The two of them might be partners and lovers. They are probably even friends, but they are not best friends. Instead of spending important time with their spouse, the other spouse is spending an exorbitant amount of time with their friends. Though they are married, they are still budgeting their time as though they are single. This is damaging to a marriage.

Single friends often complain that they lose a friend when he or she gets married. It shouldn't be true that they completely lose that friend, but it should be true that the relationship is greatly altered. Marriage changes allegiances. If a friend truly needs me but my wife needs me more, my wife gets my time.

Every relationship takes a backseat to marriage, including relationships with other family members. Spouses before children and spouses before parents.

Years ago we moved into a new house, and my mom and grandparents moved in next door. During that first week we were having dinner at my house. At one point my grandmother, mom, wife, and daughter were all in the kitchen. As I was standing there, they all told me something I should do: eat this, eat that, get more of this, get less of that.

After listening, I said, "I love all four of you, but I'm only going to take orders from one of you." It was meant as a joke, but I was still serious.

Living in close quarters to the four most important women in my life (two in my house and two next door) would be a tremendous blessing, but there was one great threat. If boundaries were not clearly drawn, confusion could exist.

While I loved all four women, my allegiance was not equally given to each of them. My relationship with my wife trumped every other one.

Far too often, husbands and wives allow their moms or dads to interfere in their relationship. The intent is well-meaning. We should always be respectful and caring toward our parents. However, boundaries must be clearly set so that everyone knows the order of priority. You can love everyone, but you have vowed your life to one person. That person must come first.

Marriage should change how we relate to family members and friends of the same sex, but it should dramatically change how we relate to friends of the opposite sex. Before marriage, there are very few rules regarding interacting with people of the opposite sex.

> *You can love everyone, but you have vowed your life to one person. That person must come first.*

At the end of a marriage seminar, I was doing a Q & A when someone asked, "How should a married man handle friendships with women?"

It was a great question, but without even thinking I gave a poor answer. I said, "They shouldn't be friends." It was a harsh answer and one I quickly changed, but it reveals an important truth.

Married men and women can be friends with one another and with their single counterparts, but those friendships should be radically different from the ones they have with people of the same sex or the relationships they had with others before they were married.

When someone desires to be married, I often give them the advice to form as many good friendships with single people of the opposite sex as possible. From these friendships, a person can determine if more might develop. Yet when a person gets married, my advice changes significantly. Marriage changes friendship.

A man and a woman cannot have the same friendship after one or both of them makes a lifelong commitment to another person. They must adapt. To keep from getting the wrong idea, giving the wrong idea, or threatening the trust of their spouse, they must draw new boundaries for their friendship. They remain friends, but the friendship is deeply altered.

There are three boundaries a married person should have with the opposite sex.

Physical Boundaries

Before marriage, two people need to draw physical boundaries. Some things should be saved solely for marriage. Yet some boundaries that single adults do not need to consider must be taken into account when one of them gets married. It's perfectly normal for two single friends to grab lunch, hang out at each other's houses, or go for a walk. It is not healthy for a married man and single woman to do those same activities. When one person pledges their life to another, new physical boundary lines must be drawn. This may be different for different people. I will not ride alone in a car with a female who is not related to me, have lunch alone with another woman (some may not be able to have this rule because of business), or go into a house when a woman is home alone.

Emotional Boundaries

Most affairs do not begin because of physical attraction; they begin because of emotional connection. When a man or woman marries another person, they must create emotional barriers with people of the opposite sex. This does not forbid the sharing of emotions with others, but it does limit what someone is willing to share. A person should never open up about the state of their marriage, their negative feelings toward their spouse, or specific struggles within their marriage to another person of the opposite sex. While it is important to talk to someone, talk to a professional, a pastor, or a friend of the same sex. Do not put yourself at risk of getting the wrong idea or sending the wrong idea to someone of the opposite sex.

Time Boundaries

While we live in a 24-7 world where the distinction between work time and family time is blurred, it is still proper to distinguish time boundaries with people of the opposite sex. Two single people can freely text one another at all hours without any questions. When one or both of those people is married, they should not have the same freedom. When and how two people communicate should be considered within the context of family time compared to work time or friend time. For example, there are normal hours for my co-workers to communicate with me. My friends have other hours. My wife and family are the only ones without any limitations. While some circumstances may require a different schedule, keeping general boundaries regarding time is healthy.

I was wrong when I told the seminar crowd they shouldn't be friends with people of the opposite sex. As I look at my own life, I can see many deeply personal relationships I have with other women. However, I approach them in a dramatically different way than I would any relationship with a man. My guard is up because I have a desire for their well-being, their families, my wife, my family, and myself.

It sounds rigid, but anyone who understands the destruction affairs can cause—anyone who has heard the heart-wrenching stories of regret or seen how preventable many of those situations were—would not consider having boundaries rigid. They would see it as a practical step to protect themselves and others.

Friendships are vital to life. A diverse set of friends brings a variety of beauty into one's life. However, we must be wise in how we deal with one another so that we can honor the vows we have made to our spouse.

How to Make Your Spouse Your Best Friend

If anyone doubts the importance of friendship when it comes to marriage, consider that most affairs begin as innocent friendships that eventually become sexual. Some begin solely to fulfill a sexual desire, but far more often a person fills a friendship void, and over time the friendship develops a physical component. Oftentimes stopping the sexual relationship is nearly impossible because the couple has formed a deep emotional bond. They have become close friends, which leads to sex.

As it is with inappropriate relationships, so it can be with proper marital relationships. While we must be careful regarding friendships with people of the opposite sex because of where it can lead, this threat should cause us to work even harder to develop a meaningful friendship with our husband or wife.

This brings us to the important question, "How can we create a friendship within our marriage?"

Sometimes it has been lost. This is a real threat for those who are in the middle of having or raising children. The demands of parenting, career, and life become so overwhelming that the friendship aspect of a marriage is ignored. It's not pushed to the side intentionally. It is simply easier to delay doing something with your spouse because of the more pressing demands of feeding your children, getting homework done, or sneaking in an extra hour of work.

At other times, friendship was never part of the marriage. When two people too quickly jump into a romantic relationship, they never develop a true friendship. The early years of their marriage are built more upon lust than love. By the time the euphoria of the new relationship wears off, they start having kids, and the next thing they know, ten years have passed and they are married to someone they have never been friends with.

In either scenario the question is the same: how do you create friendship in marriage when it currently does not exist? Here are five steps to develop it.

1. Confess to One Another That You Want More

Telling your spouse that you want a better friendship with them is a tremendous compliment. While some receive it as a criticism—as though they are not doing something right—it should be viewed as a compliment: "I love you so much I want to be closer to you." Sharing your desire to develop a deeper friendship assists each partner to hear new invitations (to activities, thoughts, or ideas) in the context of friendship, not on the surface level of an individual issue. For example, if I tell my spouse I want to develop our friendship and then later invite her on a walk, she will look past the surface issue of the walk and understand this is an activity in which we can deepen our friendship.

2. Prioritize Time to Devote to One Another

Friendship in marriage often gets pushed to the side because it isn't a pressing priority. Be an hour late for work tomorrow and you might get fired; skip your morning walk with your wife and she probably won't divorce you. Because there aren't immediate consequences when we push friendship aside, it is easy to ignore. In order to rebuild or create a friendship in marriage, time must be given to the process. By looking at the big-picture goal of a healthy marriage to their best friend, a couple can better determine what is truly important regarding their time. Tonight's ball game, the latest TV show, or a hit movie is not as important as becoming true companions with one another. Take the time to accomplish that goal.

3. Find Activities That Help You Connect

Friendship often occurs when two people engage in the same experience or activity. Consider your current friends. Chances are you met them while doing something—attending first grade, watching your kids play on the same team, or playing against one another in tennis. The activity or experience is the focus, but relationships form from the activity. The fastest way to connect with your spouse on a friendship level is to share an activity or experience. A walk is the most effective activity I'm aware of. It costs nothing, is doable for nearly every person, and requires very little planning. But as you walk, you talk. Other activities are possible—finding a new restaurant, trying new sport, or going to a concert.

Two suggestions: Choose an activity other than something that one spouse already does and the other does not. By trying his sport or doing her hobby, it creates an inequality that often doesn't lead to friendship. Also, try to make the activity something that's new or that's not in your normal routine. A new experience will help prevent you from falling into old routines of communication or thinking.

4. Lower Your Expectations

Creating a friendship in marriage is not a magical process. One experience won't forever change your relationship. If your goal is a healthy marriage that includes a significant friendship, it will take time. Like anything worth achieving, it won't necessarily be easy. Too many couples try to become friends, but after one or two experiences they give up on the process. Intention and time will result in friendship (intention + time = friendship). Take your time. Keep working. Expect success and failure. But don't expect one walk or one book to radically change your marriage.

5. Commit to Do Whatever It Takes

If you and your spouse are not close friends, it is because one or both of you have chosen not to be. You have spent your time and attention in other places. The good news is you can choose differently. Friendship is essential to a healthy marriage. Every investment you make in becoming friends with your spouse will pay off in a variety of other areas. Commit to the process of becoming friends and you will become friends.

Friendship is the foundation of marriage. Everything is built on friendship, and where it is weak, the entire stability of the relationship will be in question. For most couples, investing time in deepening their friendship with one another is the greatest thing they can do to improve their marriage. As they become better friends, they will become better partners and lovers. Improving their partnership and intimacy will make their friendship even better.

BE INTENTIONAL

1. Do you have an adequate number of friendships apart from your spouse? How can developing those relationships assist your marriage?

2. Are there any friendships you have that make your spouse uncomfortable? How should those change?

3. Think of a couple who has a marriage you admire. List three questions you would like to ask them about marriage.

4. How can you further develop your friendship with your spouse in this season of your life?

PART 2

PARTNER

7

Marry a Partner, Not a Child

Two people decide to start a business. They are going to be equal partners. This decision has consequences. It's assumed that both will do an equal amount of work, be aggressively passionate about the success of the business, and support one another in every way to make the business thrive. However, these assumptions do not mean that both will do the same type of work, always experience the exact same feelings at the same time, and have the same opinions on every issue.

When partners begin a business, they bring different strengths, abilities, and backgrounds to the table. They believe that they are better together than apart. They want to leverage their differences to the benefit of both parties. They rejoice in differences because they add strength to the organization, but their relationship is cemented by similar goals, desires, and ambitions. In partnering together, it is almost certain that both parties are in a similar life setting. Either they are both experienced businesspeople who have been around the block and have a good understanding of what is desired in their company, or they are both brand-new to the business world, idealistically believing they know how to make a company work. Either way they have chosen to tie their destinies together, trusting one another and believing they can make it together.

As it is in business, so it is in marriage. Marriage is a partnership. It is a business decision. In the past, marriage was primarily a business decision. It was not unusual in other cultures for marriage to be very little about love and very much about land, lineage, and international diplomacy. Thankfully we live in a day in which love is the main motivating factor for marriage; however, the threat for many in today's culture is to lose sight of the business side of saying "I do."

Marriage is a business. There are legal documents, tax implications, credit scores, property rights, inheritance issues, time allocation questions, income and expense reports, and job descriptions.

Marriage is a partnership. It's a business that requires two equal partners. The partnership is no less important than the friendship or the sexual connection. It can't be elevated as the centerpiece of marriage, but it also can't be pushed aside as a relic of marriages past. To deny the partnership of marriage is to deny reality. While the movies might focus more on the romance and emotional connection, a strong partnership is important to a fulfilling relationship. Without it, the couple will recognize something is missing even if they can't fully explain what it is. At its best, marriage is the partnership of two equals who use their strengths in different areas for the mutual benefit of the couple.

The Math of a Good Marriage: 1 + 1 = 3

Partnership in marriage should have a multiplying effect. It's two people coming together not just so they can accomplish the work of two, but so that now they can do the work of three. In a good marriage, the two become one, but they also remain two. They don't become one at the expense of the two; they become one in addition to the two. When marriage works, 1 + 1 = 3.

Each individual retains their individuality. Husbands and wives are as different as any two people can be. While they likely share many common goals and interests, their stories, backgrounds, perspectives, skills, and abilities differ. Those differences do not disappear at the altar. If anything, they likely become more apparent after the vows are said. Before marriage, our passion can cloud our judgment, so we downplay the differences between us and our spouse and highlight the similarities. We can fool ourselves into thinking we are identical just because the other person took the same elective as we did or went to the same concert or ate at the same restaurant.

Differences are both the source of our greatest frustration and the place of our greatest potential.

Shortly after the wedding, and hopefully somewhat before, differences begin to reveal themselves. These differences are both the source of our greatest frustration and the place of our greatest potential. When a couple can navigate the differences and appreciate them, their relationship will have a diversity of strengths and perspectives that set it up for tremendous success. However, success is dependent on the couple being able to appreciate the differences and not being driven crazy by them.

The equation for a successful marital partnership can be missed in two ways. First, some miss it because the two never become one. Each partner retains their own identity, but they never become a true couple. Each lives their own life and they never experience the power of togetherness. By themselves they can accomplish much, but they have not learned to accomplish more than what they can do on their own. In this relationship, 1 + 1 = 2. They are good, but they are only as good as two, no different than when they were single.

The second way others miss the equation is because the two *do* become one, but they lose all sense of their individual identities.

This type of relationship is tricky because the couple might believe that they have a healthy marriage. They do everything together and appear very much in love. However, they have lost their individual selves. They are unable to accomplish anything without the other. In this relationship, $1 + 1 = 1$. They are good, but they are only as good as one.

In a healthy marriage, each spouse keeps their individual identity, enjoys themselves, and accomplishes things without their partner, while also merging into a powerful partnership. They are both individuals and a couple. This is how I want my marriage to be—me, her, and us.

I am me. I exist beyond my spouse. Jenny doesn't define me. She doesn't complete me. She doesn't dictate who I am as an individual. Even without her, I'm still me. I am responsible for myself, my own happiness, my own identity, my own success in life.

She is her. She has a life beyond me. I don't define her. I don't complete her. I don't dictate who she is as an individual. Even without me, she is still her. She is responsible for herself, her own happiness, her own identity, and her own success in life.

Marriage at its best harnesses both the strength of two individuals and the power of a united couple.

Yet we are also us. We define who we are as a couple. There are things that we do together. There are aspects of our lives that are a joint venture. Without her, I don't act. Without me, she doesn't act. We have our individual things, but we also have our couple things. We hike together and run a home together. We talk with one another about the direction of her business or big issues at church. We are tennis partners and share friendships with other couples. But she never plays golf with me. While we play tennis together, she also plays in a league without me. With some couples we are friends with each spouse, but with other couples only one of us is close to them. I have my things. She has her things. And we have our things.

This is marriage at its best. It harnesses both the strength of two individuals and the power of a united couple. When any of these three aspects is not fully functioning, they all suffer. A marriage can only thrive when each spouse maintains their individual identity. Individuals can best thrive when their marriage is strong.

Marriage has a multiplying effect. We can do more together than we can do alone. While marriage might hinder aspects of what we could do individually because of demands on time and changes of affections, it greatly multiplies what we can do together.

When a Spouse Becomes a Child

Gary and Shelly look like the perfect couple. Both are outgoing and engaging and seem deeply in love. Their dating story was textbook. After the perfect wedding and a few years of newlywed bliss, they started having children. First a daughter and then a son were added to the house.

As a nurse, Shelly is gone from the kids more than she wants, but she is a great mother and wife. Her absence requires Gary to play an active role as a father, which he embraces well. Other than the perfect ponytail, there is nothing Gary can't do for his kids. Others call him "Mr. Mom," but he always shakes his head and says, "It's actually called being a father." Many see Gary as the perfect husband, but Shelly doesn't feel that way. She knows he is good in many areas, but there is one frustration she can't shake. Gary can never hold down a job, and it's not because of companies downsizing due to shipping jobs overseas or because of technology making his field of expertise irrelevant. Gary can't keep a job because he refuses to do the work necessary. He is lazy and a bit entitled, and he either thinks he is too good for a job or simply enjoys Shelly taking care of him.

Every time he gets a job, she hopes this will be the one. But every time, there is an excuse—the boss is too demanding, the schedule isn't fair, the job doesn't match his dream. There is always a reason for him to quit. He has never been fired, as far as she knows. But the truth is, he has been forced out of nearly every job because of his bad attitude, excuse making, or poor work ethic.

If you ask Gary, he is a great husband. He will admit he has struggled with his career, but he will quickly point out how much housework he does, the amount of time he spends with the kids, how beloved he is by everyone, and how often he covers for Shelly as proof he is living by his vows.

Shelly would tell a different story. She raves about the type of father Gary is. She still loves him and considers him her best friend. But she will hesitate if you ask, "Is he a good husband?" She considers herself lucky in many areas because of Gary, but she is weary from the pressure of being the sole breadwinner. She's tired of having to play the role of Gary's mom when it comes to telling him he can't spend money whenever he wants or needs to put in another job application. She looks at her friends whose husbands go to work every day, and she is jealous. But it's not because of the job. A friend of Gary and Shelly's was recently laid off. Shelly watched as he had several interviews the next week. He was working hard to get a new job. That's all Shelly wants from Gary. Work to get a job, and when you get it, keep it. But Gary refuses. He is a great friend and lover, but Gary is failing Shelly because he is not an equal partner.

That's not to say he has to have a job to be an equal partner. If Gary and Shelly came to the joint conclusion that Shelly's job could support the family and they want Gary to stay home to be a full-time dad, there would be nothing wrong with that choice. But that is not what they have decided. It is what Gary has decided without the blessing of Shelly. And it is damaging their marriage.

When one spouse refuses to play their equal role in the partnership of marriage, the dynamics of the relationship shift to parent/child. This relationship is meaningful when it takes place between a parent and child. It isn't equal—the power structure is clearly tilted so the parent has power and the child is expected to submit. This is for the benefit of the child. It is in their best interest to have a parent rule over them. In marriage, a parent/child relationship is destructive.

I love my children, but they are not equal partners in the family. They are equal *participants*, but not partners. They are not expected to contribute in the same way that their mother and I contribute. They do not feel the stress and strain that comes from being an equal partner. They have a right to assume many things will simply happen without their effort. Food will be in the pantry, the bills will be paid, and their mother and I will do everything in our power to provide the basic necessities they need for success. They participate in the family, but they are not equal partners.

As they age, my expectations for them will increase, and when they are capable of being an equal partner, they will be expected to move out and start their own homes. Before that time, they will not have the capacity to handle the pressure. Even if they could, I would not want them to experience it. I want them to be children—to enjoy the benefits of their parents' labor and allow us to do the work necessary to provide for them.

What we want for our children, we do not want for our spouse. It is our rightful expectation that a spouse will play an equal role in the ownership of the family. It doesn't mean both spouses will have jobs outside of the house or perform the exact same tasks. It does mean they will be equally involved in energy and effort toward the well-being of the partnership.

Too many marriages devolve into a parent-child relationship. One spouse plays the role of the parent:

They see the big picture.

They make the tough decisions.

They prevent the other spouse from doing foolish things.

The other spouse plays the role of the child:

They hide things from their mate.

They are more focused on having fun than reaching long-term goals.

They do not carry their share of the workload or responsibility.

On paper these are marriages, but in practice they are replicas of the relationship that one spouse had with their mom or dad. This dynamic comes in two forms: chronic parent/child relationships and situational parent/child relationships.

Chronic Parent/Child Relationships

Some marriages are stuck in a chronic parent/child relationship. While it may not define the whole marriage, it can describe a continual pattern of interaction in one or multiple areas of life. Often it begins at a young age. The couple gets married, and before kids there are very few things off-limits regarding time and energy. As time passes and responsibilities increase, a healthy couple changes and matures, whereas an unhealthy couple does not. One spouse may transition, but the other remains stuck.

Before kids, it's not an issue when a wife wants to hang out with her girlfriends after work. But when kids come along and the nights out are too frequent, a husband can begin to feel like a single dad putting his kids to bed as he worries about his wife making it home. Similarly, a lot of guys play video games through high school and college. The games often transition to the couple's first house. It's not a problem to play video games, but when it takes the central place in the husband's life rather than being a rare way to blow off steam, the wife can feel isolated. In these scenarios, it is not unusual for the husband to try to restrict how many times the wife can go out with her friends, or for the wife to limit the amount of time a husband can play video games. In the first scenario, the husband is playing the role of a dad, and in the second situation, the wife is being her husband's mom. The relationship is not equal.

In chronic parent/child relationships, both spouses have work to do. One spouse needs to grow up. I often find myself looking a husband in the eye and telling him, "Your wife deserves a husband, not a child. Start being a man." After I hear the couple describe what is taking place, it becomes obvious the husband is not playing his part. He is distracted by a hobby or a game or some other area in which he is using his strengths for himself and his own enjoyment rather than for the well-being of the couple and the nourishment of the family. In these cases, I plead with the man to be a man. His wife deserves a full partner, not another dependent. He needs to do his job. He needs to support the family financially, be responsible, stop making foolish decisions, act his age, pick up his things, share the household chores, stop trying to make a career out of a hobby, save money instead of spending it, and do a host of other commonsense actions that a partner in a business relationship would assume is normal.

Yet the other spouse has work to do as well. They need to stop being the parent. Oftentimes when I tell a person they need to stop parenting their spouse, they respond by saying, "But if I don't, who will?" In the same way that their spouse needs to stop acting like a child, they need to stop acting like a parent. This doesn't mean that they put the children in danger or make foolish financial decisions or risk the well-being of the family. It does mean they do what they are supposed to do and stop doing what their spouse should do. While there is no excuse for a spouse to play the role of a child, one reason many do is because they have been allowed to without any real consequences. So the active alcoholic or relapsed prescription drug user or the wannabe rock star can ignore their family and their responsibilities without experiencing homelessness, separation from their children, or an end to the intimate relationship with their spouse.

Why should they grow up if they never experience the negative consequences of their decisions? If the worst thing that happens to them is an occasional cold shoulder or huff from their spouse, there isn't a driving reason for them to stop drinking, come home on time, or get a job. While it is unhealthy, the parent/child relationship is often pretty comfortable for the "child." Everything of importance gets taken care of for them without any effort on their part. They might have to put up with some complaining from the "parent," but the complaining often goes in one ear and out the other. In the end, the bills are paid, food is on the table, and they get to continue in their childish ways. They will continue until the "parent" stops being the parent and starts being the spouse. It may not change the "child," but it is the only chance they have of changing.

While it is unhealthy, the parent/child relationship is often pretty comfortable for the "child."

I was always told Mary was sick. Her husband was a saint in my eyes. He served his wife in a way I can't even begin to imagine. For decades he worked, cleaned, cooked, and did everything in between. She did very little, but she was sick. To the shock of everyone, Mary's husband suddenly died one day. It was a tragic loss. There was a great debate about what would happen to Mary. Maybe she could move in with one of the kids, or maybe she needed to go into assisted living. No one was certain, but everyone knew she couldn't make it on her own. Until she did.

To everyone's surprise, Mary was able to do everything required to live on her own. She cooked for the first time in years. She cleaned house. She took care of herself. Come to find out, she had been able to the whole time, but no one knew her ability because her husband always waited on her. When he was no longer there, either she could do things for herself or she would have to move into assisted living. So she took care of herself. Obviously, it was possible that Mary wouldn't have been able to take care of herself, but no one would have known her capability had death not stopped her husband from doing everything.

As it was with Mary, so it is with every spouse who is playing the role of the child. Until they are forced to be an adult, they will simply continue being a child. But when the "parent" stops parenting, the "child" will have a choice. Sadly, some choose to continue down an immature path, but others get the wake-up call they need and start playing the role they were supposed to play.

Situational Parent/Child Relationships

While some couples are stuck in a chronic parent/child relationship, nearly every couple will face moments in which they are tempted to act within the parent/child framework. This temptation will derive from either our fear of responsibility or our need for control.

Being an adult is hard. Responsibilities grow at a pace that often exceeds confidence. There are moments in which nearly every adult desires to tap out of all the demands and have someone take care of them. One of the great privileges of marriage is knowing we always have someone who has our back. If a sudden flu hits a wife, she should be encouraged to know that for at least forty-eight hours her husband can cover everything that needs to be done to keep the home running.

At our best, we will use this privilege as little as necessary, but at our worst, we may exploit our spouse for our personal gain. Sometimes we drop the ball because we know someone else is there to pick it up. Out of laziness, boredom, or just selfishness, we are tempted to ignore our responsibilities as a husband or wife, which obligates our spouse to carry more of the load than they should. This temptation should be rebuked at every turn.

Yet the more likely scenario for us is to take on the parenting role, because with it comes the perception of control. With good intentions, a husband can "parent" his wife because he thinks he is doing what is best for her. Or a wife, while meaning to do what is best, can "parent" her husband, not realizing she is stripping him of his humanity and adulthood.

Nagging is a bad parenting technique, yet many wives use it against their husbands. It is often joked of as a natural part of marriage, but it is not an aspect of a healthy relationship. It is a way in which one spouse is trying to control the other, and it tips the power structure of the relationship.

Work and parenting can drive us into a parent/child relationship without us recognizing it. Both Jenny and I have found ourselves telling the other what to do, unaware we are treating each other the way we treat our children. We wake up in the morning and do everything in our power to get our kids out of the house and to school. We are shouting orders to both children. Then we head to work, where we are striving toward a goal and convincing other people to go in the direction we think they need to go. We come home to once again corral the kids through homework and bedtime.

In the midst of the average day, we are making many decisions and telling a lot of people what to do. It is not unusual for us to use the same technique with one another. Yet Jenny is not my child. I am not her employee. In most of our daily relationships, there is a clear line of reporting. One person works for another, or one person is the child of another. But in marriage, there is no power structure between Jenny and me. We are equal not only in personhood but also in authority, responsibility, and expectation. We often laugh when one of us gives an order to the other in the same tone we might give to one of our children. We catch ourselves wading into a parent/child relationship without even realizing we are doing so. In the same way that we must guard against acting like a child instead of an adult, we must also make sure that we treat our spouse like an adult rather than a child.

The Power of an Equal Relationship

While we are tempted to devolve into a parent/child relationship, there is nothing better than an equal relationship between two loving adults. Partnership, at its very best, empowers each individual to experience their full potential while encouraging them to know that in times of weakness, there is always someone who has their back.

Partnership allows a spouse to try new things, stretch their boundaries, and explore unknown places because of the stability of the relationship. It reassures us that in failure and success we will have someone to weep with us or cheer us on. It challenges us to live day to day with another adult who is striving to do the best they can. It gives us the opportunity to use every aspect of who we are for the well-being of another person. It reveals to us our greatest weaknesses and needs, all within the comfort of a loving, lasting relationship. It changes who we are and what we want, drawing us out of ourselves and making us passionate about the success of the one we love. It teaches us about ourselves and others, instructing us in ways we would never learn on our own. It presents to us the capacity to affect and influence many more people and circumstances than we could on our own.

> *Partnership, at its very best, empowers each individual to experience their full potential while encouraging them to know that in times of weakness, there is always someone who has their back.*

Marriage between two equal adults is far too rich to be squandered away in a parent/child relationship. I love my parents, but I don't need more than the two I have. I love my children and am content with both of them. I do not need another mom or daughter. I need Jenny to be my wife. It's a role no one else can play—my equal in every respect, neither over me nor under me, neither further ahead nor a little behind. She is my partner. She is the one who has my back.

BE INTENTIONAL

1. Why does the partnership of marriage feel less important than the friendship or intimacy?

2. Marriage has a multiplying effect. What are some ways your spouse multiplies your capabilities?

3. Is there any area within your marriage in which you operate with a parent/child relationship? How is each of you contributing to that unhealthy dynamic?

4. What most makes you feel as though your spouse has your back?

8

How I Predict Divorce Based on the Wedding Cake

I officiated my first wedding before I had my first kiss. While I possessed the authority to bind two people together in holy matrimony, I struggled with the ability to ask a friend to the movies. Asking her to accompany me to a wedding was easier.

So at one of the first weddings I performed, I asked a girl to join me. The ceremony went off without a hitch. Following the nuptials, I was enjoying some punch and talking to my date as the couple cut the cake. As the bride did the cutting, the groom began to joke and she began to joke back. Behind their smiles was a seriousness few saw. He was threatening to smash the cake in her face. She was letting him know that she wouldn't hesitate to do the same. The groom then fed the cake to his bride with a bit more force than I would recommend. She responded with equal aggressiveness. When he reciprocated, the fight was on. Within seconds, the couple went to the ground, attempting to force cake into each other's face.

I turned to my friend and asked, "Is this normal?" Having attended more weddings than me, she replied, "I don't think so."

Two decades and a few hundred weddings later, I always watch the wedding cake exchange with great interest. Show me how a couple feeds one another wedding cake, and I can make a pretty decent guess on whether or not that couple will have a marriage that includes respect. Does he respect her enough not to embarrass her? Does she respect him enough not to emasculate him? Do they respect one another enough not to retaliate if the other uses more force than appropriate? Do they playfully interact with one another? Is someone willing to deflate the situation if it gets tense?

Weddings are unique events for several reasons, but one of the most unusual aspects of a wedding is the couple being in the spotlight. Most of us live our lives in anonymity. A few people see us, but we don't regularly operate on stage. Crowds can make people do crazy things. A crowd can't make us do something we would never do, but it can encourage us to do things we would rarely do—such as tackle our new wife to the ground in an attempt to get a laugh.

Respect is a necessary ingredient for a successful marriage. It is a prerequisite for a healthy partnership. When respect is absent, a husband and wife cannot be true partners. They might be great friends. They might have moments of sexual chemistry. But they will not be true life partners who are confident that their spouse always has their back.

We respect people's strengths. This doesn't happen in denial of their weaknesses, but it is the result of seeing those imperfections within a larger context of abilities, aptitudes, and skills.

Unhealthy relationships do not necessarily have more character flaws or inabilities. More often they have the same strengths and weaknesses as any couple, but one or both spouses have established the destructive habit of fixating on the negative. When spouses define each other by their weaknesses, respect is quickly lost. We allow our spouse's weaknesses to eclipse their every strength. Instead of viewing a weakness as one aspect of who they are or a downside to a positive quality, we strip the person of their humanity and define them as stupid, evil, or below us. No longer seeing them as our equal, we pity them, hate them, or simply stop thinking about them. When respect is lost, the partnership is dissolved. When it is present and developed, the partnership thrives.

What It Means to Me

One of the most important questions we can ask ourselves and our spouse regarding respect is, "How do you feel it?" Respecting my spouse is vital, but I want to make sure she *feels* valued. What are the ways in which she best receives my communication of respect? When I show it in a way that speaks to her heart, it is important that she communicates that feeling to me. Similarly, I must recognize the moments in which I feel most appreciated by my spouse and communicate those moments to her.

People feel respect in different ways. By communicating our feelings, we empower our spouse to act in a way that will speak best to us. Equally important, we must communicate circumstances in which we feel disrespected by our spouse. These are often easier to recognize. I often tell couples, "Describe something your spouse does that feels disrespectful to you." If the couple feels safe enough, they can normally list off something:

"When he just sets his dirty dish on the counter, expecting me to clean it."

"When she cuts me off when I'm talking."

"When he doesn't recognize I've had a bad day."

"When she doesn't give me time to collect myself after work."

"When he won't tell his mother no and just expects me to go along."

"When she tells me I can't do something, as though I'm a child."

In all these examples, the actions taken are received as a very specific communication: *You do not value me as an individual*. A healthy couple can communicate about those moments and learn how to build respect. Unhealthy couples refuse to communicate, or if they do communicate, they refuse to apply their knowledge and change their actions.

Respect Means I See You

At its heart, respect is recognizing another person and valuing what we see. The prerequisite demands that I see you. I can't respect what I don't see. To respect my spouse, I must see what is going on in her life. Friendship fuels partnership because it gives us a deeper understanding of our spouse, which causes us to better understand who they are and what is happening in their lives.

At the core of most disrespect is a failure to see our spouse. We don't understand the needs in their lives or how our actions impact them. Most people do not desire to be disrespectful. A lack of respect is rarely born out of intention but is more often the result of ignorance. We act in selfish ways, unknowingly hurting those around us. In order for me to see you, I also have to see me. I have to understand the consequences of my actions and how they impact those around me.

Every day ask each other, "What is one way I can help you today?"

One of the most effective ways to develop respect for our spouse is by taking intentional steps to understand their needs and how we can assist them. I often encourage couples to try the following exercise for two weeks. Every day ask each other, "What is one way I can help you today?"

This doesn't guarantee that you will be able to do what they ask. It does not obligate you to the task unless you specifically say that you will do it. But it does inform you of what is taking place in your spouse's day and helps you understand at least one way you can shoulder part of the burden for your spouse.

If a couple will ask this question, several things will occur:

They will better understand what is taking place in their spouse's life.

They will more likely assist their spouse during the day.

They will be more likely to consider other things they can do to help their spouse.

They will not feel alone in the demands of their day.

They will experience gratitude when their spouse has the ability to help them.

They will find themselves thinking more about their spouse on a daily basis.

All of these have a positive impact on our marriages. We learn to depend on each other and cultivate a deeper respect as partners.

Communication and Respect

Respect creates good communication, and good communication deepens respect. If I respect my spouse, I will

want to know her

want to be known by her

be willing to listen

give her the attention she needs to communicate to me

refuse to make any assumptions regarding her opinions or ideas

not belittle her

not caricature her (e.g., "all women are emotional")

understand she is a complex person whom I do not fully know

speak *to* her and not *at* her

listen when spoken to

give her ample time for communication to take place

clearly show my desire for her to communicate with me

reveal my heart to her

While respect is an internal feeling of admiration, it expresses itself through action. A person can't claim to respect their spouse if their actions do not clearly reveal that. Yet acting respectfully is the best way to grow feelings of respect.

Having a temporary disagreement or miscommunication is not evidence of an absence of respect; it is evidence of two different people trying to understand one another. However, if there is a pattern that proves communication is difficult regarding an issue, the root problem is likely a lack of respect.

Can't talk about money? Do you respect the financial decisions of your spouse?

Can't talk about sex? Do you respect the sexual desires of your spouse?

Can't talk about kids? Do you respect your spouse as a parent?

When certain topics are off-limits between a couple, it is likely a sign that respect is lacking in that area. Where a lack of communication indicates a lack of respect, good communication can often rebuild the trust.

Jeremy and Sarah cannot talk about money. Every time they begin the discussion, a fight breaks out. The issue is that Sarah doesn't respect Jeremy when it comes to money. She pays the bills, knows the bank balance, and tries to save a little money toward retirement. Jeremy simply spends money. While their relationship is strong in many areas, money is the main area of frustration. Time has taught them to ignore the issue in order to avoid a fight. Yet ignoring topics is not the pathway to a healthy relationship. For a meaningful partnership to develop, Jeremy and Sarah need to learn how to communicate about the topic without arguing. They don't have to agree, but they do need to negotiate a working plan of action that can be revisited when the issue needs to be discussed.

If the couple has a strong friendship, it can assist their partnership. When communication about an issue is difficult, the issue is normally within the partnership of the relationship. But instead of discussing it like partners, a healthy couple can discuss it like friends.

Friends listen. They don't judge. They don't condemn. They are more concerned with hearing their friend's heart than persuading their friend to think exactly like them. This is why it is often easy to communicate with friends. Friends communicate respectfully—no name calling, no shame, no judgment, empathic listening, and a true desire to understand what the other person thinks and feels.

Too often, couples fail to communicate like friends. Instead, they attack one another, attempting to win the argument and get their way. Disrespect describes many conversations. One possible response to disrespect is avoidance. If Jeremy and Sarah would learn how to communicate respectfully about money, they may not agree on the issue, but they could find a workable framework for handling their monthly finances. The issue will likely always be one of contention, but respectful communication can help them better understand one another and prevent them from making disrespectful statements about each other (e.g., "All she cares about is money" or "He is so irresponsible").

Respectful communication would likely lead to actual respect about the issue of money. If Jeremy heard Sarah communicate her feelings about money—how she worries, her dreams for the future, her hard work concerning the family finances—he may better understand why she gets frustrated about his spending. He might then begin to respect her regarding finances, whereas in the past he has not.

Respectful communication does the following:

It recognizes the humanity of the other person.

It refuses to make judgmental statements.

It clearly communicates personal feelings.

It patiently listens.

It says "I," not "you."

It stays on topic.

It speaks in an appropriate tone.

The Lowest Bar for Marital Success

Within communication and the relationship in general, there is a low bar to gauge the respect in your marriage, a good measuring stick to keep in mind: do you treat your spouse with at least the same amount of respect and dignity you show to others?

That shouldn't be the bar we use for our actions within marriage. The goal should be much higher. Yet it is a simple test we can give ourselves when it comes to the issue of respect. I regularly speak with couples who describe how they speak and act toward one another in private, and I am shocked. They never treat me the way they describe. With me they show respect, kindness, and restraint, but with one another they are rude, vile, and demanding. It's an ugly hypocrisy.

Do you treat your spouse with at least the same amount of respect and dignity you show to others?

Respect demands that we not treat our spouse worse than we treat others. Without question we can let our guard down with our spouse. We do not have to put on an act as we often do with others. However, if letting our guard down means being a jerk, we need to put the guard back up. If we treat our spouse in a way we would never treat a stranger, we are not respecting them. Our spouse does not have a right to expect perfection from us, yet they do have the right to generally expect the best from us. We have no right to treat others kindly and then be consistently rude with our spouse. It is wrong to help everyone else we meet but then regularly fail to assist our spouse with their life. If I would never yell at a co-worker, demean a friend, or be rude to a cashier, then I should never yell at, demean, or be rude to my wife. And if I do, I would hope that I would recognize it, apologize, and change my actions.

Many couples fail to have a healthy partnership because they treat their partner in a way they would never treat anyone else in their lives. They give their best to others but their worst to their spouse. It is a failure of respect.

Consider this: If you treated your spouse while you were dating the way you treat them now, would they have ever agreed to marry you? Who thinks you are a better man—your wife or a waitress? Who respects you more—your husband or a co-worker?

We often use the phrase "common courtesy." It is a general understanding of how people deserve to be treated no matter who they are, what they are doing, or how you happen to interact with them. Common courtesy begins at home, with a basic level of respect, dignity, restraint, and trust. Without it, we are doomed to fail. With it, we can begin to build a relationship that lasts.

Emotional and Physical

The presence of respect drives a couple to nourish both an emotional and a physical relationship with one another. It is too simplistic to think of these categories solely in traditional gender ways, as though every woman must have an emotional connection and every man needs a physical connection to feel respected. Both partners need both connections.

However, the stereotypes are present for a reason. As a general rule, more men feel respected when the physical relationship is

healthy. Without a healthy physical intimacy, many men will struggle to believe their spouse respects them. Men often intermingle
respect and desire. A wife can deeply respect her husband, but if
she fails to respect his physical needs, her words will be empty.
For most men, an intimate physical connection is the way they
experience a meaningful emotional connection.

Many women separate the two. An emotional connection is a
prerequisite for a physical connection. This is why a man must pursue an emotional connection with his wife outside the bedroom. It
communicates a true respect for who she is as a person, not simply
what she can give him sexually. When a husband nourishes the emotional connection with his wife, she feels valued and appreciated.

Notice how in a healthy marriage, each aspect—friend, partner,
and lover—feeds the others. When spouses develop a meaningful
partnership based on respect, it feeds their friendship. Respect
drives the couple to nourish a healthy emotional connection, which
strengthens the friendship bond. That same respect causes the
couple to recognize the physical needs each experiences and ensures they will not deny those needs. The partnership enhances
their intimate life because they recognize differences, celebrate
strengths and weaknesses, and feel a close bond with one another
as they live life together.

Disrespect doesn't just hinder the partnership; it stunts growth
in every aspect of marriage. Where respect is present, any struggle
can be overcome because both partners are willing to humbly attack the problem and strengthen the marriage.

Respect Determines Influence

When respect is present, both partners influence one another, improving each individual and strengthening the relationship. When
respect is absent, influence ceases. If I can neither influence my
partner nor be influenced by her, I am not receiving the maximum

benefit from a healthy marriage. A healthy marriage makes us better. It calls from us our very best as we assist our partner. It invests into us the very best as our partner makes us better.

Joe and Judy have been married for over four decades. Judy stayed home to raise the kids as Joe made a career in banking. He worked his way up to be the president of one bank and then spent the last chapter of his career building a new bank. Over the years, Joe hired a lot of employees. Some were great successes and others did not work out so well. But not a single key hire was made without that person meeting Judy. Why?

Judy never worked a single day as a teller, lender, or vice president. She didn't study bank regulations or have a degree in marketing. If she had applied for any of the jobs for which Joe was hiring, she would never have been considered because of her lack of experience. So why did she play such an influential role in the hiring process? While Judy didn't know banking, she did know Joe. Better than anyone, she knew his strengths, weaknesses, tendencies, and blind spots. She knew the process when Joe succeeded and the reasons for many of his failures. She had forty years of experience listening to him struggle when an employee wasn't working out. It was Joe's job to make sure the candidate had the banking skills necessary for a position. It was Judy's job to give a second opinion on the candidate as a person. More importantly, she was there to protect Joe from himself.

> *The ultimate test of respect between two spouses can be defined by a single question: "Do I allow my spouse to influence me?"*

The ultimate test of respect between two spouses can be defined by a single question: "Do I allow my spouse to influence me?" If the answer is no, it is proof we do not respect our spouse.

Those we admire impact us. We change because of who they are and what they believe about us. A little kid idolizes an all-star baseball player. Before long the kid tries to walk, dress, and play like him. If the major leaguer wears his hat with a flat bill, so does the kid. If he puts black under his eye, so does the kid. If he sleeps with his bat, so does the kid.

When we respect someone's skill, ability, or knowledge, we allow them to change how we think, believe, or act. Healthy couples deeply influence one another in every area of life. Consider these questions:

Are you influenced by your spouse?

How has your spouse made you a better man or woman?

How has your spouse positively affected you as a parent?

How does your spouse assist your career?

What is a daily habit you formed because of your spouse?

What is something you have stopped because your spouse showed you a better way?

Good partners influence one another. That influence is a by-product of respect.

Smash the Cake If You Wish

It's not the average phone call that I receive. "Is it okay if I smash cake in my wife's face?" he asked. He explained how he and his fiancée had read about my wedding cake prediction technique and were disappointed. They wanted a good marriage, but they also wanted to have a royal battle when cutting their wedding cake.

I laughed and asked him, "Are you serious?"

He said, "Yes."

"Then smash it," I said. "As long as you have talked about it, are certain what the other person wants, and are on the same page, it doesn't matter what you do."

The issue isn't the cake. If two people want to put on a show for those in attendance, they can battle it out. Even as they are shoving icing up their noses, they can show respect for one another. Similarly, another couple can kindly exchange cake, all the while masking a complete lack of respect for each other. Predicting divorce based on a wedding cake exchange is silly. It's an officiate's game played to break the monotony of overseeing wedding after wedding. It is probably as predictable as monkeys picking stocks or puppies picking the winner of the Super Bowl.

But the premise isn't silly. What I saw years ago, I've seen in many weddings since. Beyond the cake exchange, I regularly see couples interacting in a way that reveals the absence of respect between them—an expert giving a speech who mocks his wife in exchange for an easy laugh; the woman in the stands who belittles her husband in order to get sympathy from her friends; the man who always answers his phone no matter what the situation, except when his wife is calling.

Disrespect reveals itself in subtle ways. It is often easier to see it in others than ourselves. But respect is vital. Without it, a couple cannot develop a true partnership. Respect for my wife causes me to trust her ability to hold up her end of the relationship and reminds me of her worthiness, which helps me do the work necessary to hold up my end. Where respect is absent, individuals find their spouses neither able nor worthy. Where it is present, both ability and value are held in high esteem.

BE INTENTIONAL

1. How do you show respect for your spouse, and how do you most feel respected by them?

2. What are some ways your spouse communicates disrespect toward you?

3. What are some positive ways in which your spouse has influenced you?

4. How has the issue of respect revealed itself in your sexual relationship?

9

Why Nobel Peace Prize Winners Get Divorced

Why do Nobel Peace Prize winners get divorced? Nelson Mandela, Henry Kissinger, Kofi Annan, Shimon Peres, and others have been awarded the prestigious award for negotiating peace between countries where it seemed impossible. But they were not able to make peace with a person they shared life with. They were able to navigate the subtle dance of international diplomacy but were not able to figure out how to lie in bed at night with the same woman for a lifetime.

If they couldn't have lasting marriages, is it any surprise to us when we struggle in our own marriages?

We often think of marriage as the holy matrimony of two completely compatible individuals. In reality a husband and wife are two completely different people—with different experiences, different backgrounds, different genetic makeups, and different expectations—trying to live life together. Conflict is guaranteed. While we shouldn't seek it, we should embrace it, because making peace in the midst of conflict is important in marriage.

Good partners develop a key skill that benefits the whole marriage. They learn to negotiate. Many consider the word *negotiate* to be a negative term. Unhealthy couples are skeptical of the negotiation process because they do not trust their partner. Their defenses are up as they fear they might be taken advantage of. Healthy couples are not afraid of negotiation. They understand it is a natural part of being married. Trusting that their spouse has the couple's best interests at heart and respects their problem-solving skills, a happy couple negotiates everything.

In Latin, the word *negotiate* originally meant "to do business." Over time the word took on its current meaning: "communicating in hopes of creating mutual agreement." Few things would qualify as a more important aspect of marriage than that.

The task of marriage is to find common ground in the midst of differences. To choose battles and fight them fairly. To lock arms and attack problems instead of attacking one another. To be changed by our spouse for the good while also giving them the time and space to be changed.

At the heart of partnership is negotiation. And the purpose of negotiation is to make peace. Whenever I think about a marriage in its ideal state, I think of a couple at peace. That doesn't mean they are in total agreement. It doesn't mean they are of the same opinion. It does mean whatever issues might be between them are at rest. They have navigated the rough waters to find a calm place they both can accept.

Peace is made. It is struggled for and fought for. It is attained through hard work, sacrifice, energy, and effort. It is not something that magically happens. Peacemaking, not peace receiving, is a key aspect of marriage.

Friction is a guaranteed aspect of marriage. Psychologist John Gottman gives couples one of the greatest insights into marriage they can know. He reminds them that 70 percent of all problems are not solvable. They are perpetual problems that are sourced in differing opinions, backgrounds, or perspectives that do not have a definite right or wrong. Spouses must navigate these issues, find a workable solution, and accept that differing opinions will always be present.

Rather than fixing these perpetual conflicts, healthy couples continually communicate about them and negotiate a solution that finds mutual agreement.

How to Handle Friction in Marriage

The earth's surface is in constant motion. Immense rigid plates are always moving. Some are moving away from each other, others are running into each other, and many are sliding underneath one another with constant force. When two plates are in contact with each other, friction builds. Energy is stored. Eventually, the energy is released, resulting in an earthquake. Many are never felt. Some are a gentle rumble. But a few terrify anyone who experiences them.

Plate tectonics not only explains earthquakes, but it also serves as a good explanation of marriage—rigid people always in motion, often running into each other, resulting in friction. It cannot be avoided. As much as we like to think we are moving in the same direction and should seek to move in the same direction, we cannot be of the same mind or motivation on every issue. Because of our differences—in experiences, passions, expectations, and desires—we will often move in a direction opposite of our spouse. The result is friction.

Left unchanged, friction will build until it is released. When it comes to handling friction, couples take different approaches.

Some try to avoid it. Just as some of the earth's plates are moving away from each other, many couples are in the process of moving away from one another. The good news is that these couples do not have much friction. The bad news is that they don't have much of anything. Two people who are emotionally moving away from one another will soon physically move away from each other, and the relationship will end. While avoiding friction is appealing, it is a dangerous solution that never results in a healthy marriage.

Some try to ignore it. As major earthquakes are a part of life, many couples have come to believe they are also a part of marriage, so they do nothing about it. They ignore the issues that cause friction, allowing energy to build. Most of the time the energy is released in minor fights, but on occasion enough energy builds for an all-out explosion, which terrifies everyone around. This is a common state for many marriages. Some couples go through a major earthquake early in their marriage and quickly conclude that the first option—avoiding friction—is the best solution. Others enter into a repeating cycle of colliding into one another, letting the friction build, and having another explosion. The result is contention, instability, and the ever-looming question of "When will the Big One occur?"

Thankfully there is a third option to dealing with friction in marriage. Some couples do something about it. They know collisions cannot be avoided in a healthy marriage, but they also feel the power to influence their relationship enough to make a difference.

The first step to handling friction is to inundate your relationship with mercy. The giving and receiving of mercy eases the tension in marriage. Mercy is the grease that minimizes the friction. It is what allows us to deal with the difficult issues without an explosion. It is what gives us courage to move toward instead of away from each other. It is what makes marriage possible.

Without mercy, the struggles will be too much. Every issue would hold the potential of being destructive. The daily giving and receiving of mercy between spouses is vital for a happy marriage.

I need to give mercy. I cannot expect anyone to be perfect, including my spouse. Failure on the part of my spouse is not a sign that she does not love me; it is a reminder that she is a fallible human being. She deserves the widest strike zone I can give. If I can offer mercy to anyone, my spouse deserves it first.

I need to receive mercy. I should be quick to give mercy because I know my own need for it. I am not perfect. I cannot be perfect. I will fail every day. I need to be quick to admit my faults and receive mercy from others, especially my spouse. Receiving mercy is not a sign of weakness but is a recognition of my true need.

Within the framework of mercy, friction can be endured.

The Number One Rule of Disagreement: Do Not Make It Personal

As mercy is given and received, a couple can have the courage to confront issues as they arise rather than letting them build. When it comes to disagreement, there is one major difference between healthy relationships and unhealthy ones. It is not the amount of disagreement that occurs. Healthy couples often face just as much friction as unhealthy ones. The difference is how the disagreements are handled.

I am no stranger to disagreement. On a regular basis I encounter people extremely upset by something I've written or said. Some are effective critiques that cause me to evaluate my own opinion and often strengthen my relationship with the person even if we do not end up with the same perspective. Others are damaging events that cause me to more firmly believe my words and distance myself from the person raising the issue.

There is only one difference between the two: whether or not the person makes the criticism personal. When they criticize an idea, I'm open to the discussion and quickly review my position with the possibility of changing my mind. Yet when someone criticizes me—my heart, intelligence, or intent—I quickly shut down, doubting the person's sincerity and concept. The number one rule of disagreement is, do not make it personal.

Healthy partners fight about issues. They hold deep-seated opinions and passionately engage their partners in discussion about those issues. They are seeking the best resolution and do not easily cede their side. But they are focused on the issue.

Unhealthy partners fight about each other. They are unwilling to separate ideas from people, positions of the mind from the heart of the person. Every argument becomes about who they are as a person. It is a battle not to defend their idea but to defend their heart, mind, and soul.

There is a distinct difference between someone discussing an issue and someone defending their honor. When couples confront problems as problems rather than people, they remain on the same side. It is them against the problem. While they each may have differing opinions on how to solve it, they are united in their attempt to find common ground.

Healthy partners fight about issues. Unhealthy partners fight about each other.

When couples confront problems as people, they become opponents. Instead of fighting *with* each other, they fight *against* each other. It becomes a battle that only one spouse can win, which guarantees the couple will lose.

How do we keep from making disagreements personal? One way is to intentionally choose the right words.

Use Hard Words, Not Harsh Words

Love demands difficult conversations. Issues cannot be ignored. Feelings must be communicated, opinions must be presented, and frustrations must be expressed. For any improvement, difficult conversations must take place. As they do, wise couples use hard words, not harsh words. They aren't afraid to say what needs to be said. They don't hesitate to communicate. They put the welfare of others above personal comfort. They say hard things, such as,

"I'm not happy."

"I didn't like that decision."

"I disagree."

"I was wrong."

"Will you forgive me?"

Because these are hard words, most people avoid them. But the issues still remain. If they're not confronted, frustrations grow, negative consequences increase, and tensions fester. Eventually, conflict erupts and the hidden feelings explode to the surface. And in the passionate confrontation, hard words often give way to harsh words. Instead of discussing the issue, a couple attacks one another. They blame, injure, assault, and attempt to win the argument at all costs—even the dignity and personhood of their spouse.

Hard words provide an opportunity to expose a problem and fix it; harsh words distract from the issue and focus on a person. The harshest words normally begin with the word "you":

"You think . . ."

"You always . . ."

"You feel . . ."

"You never . . ."

"You are a . . ."

The word "you" often stops communication. It defines the other person without allowing them to define themselves. It injures, labels, and demeans.

The hardest word to say is "I," because it requires us to reveal our true thoughts and feelings. It demands reflection and honesty.

"I feel . . ."

"I think . . ."

"I believe . . ."

"I want . . ."

"I will . . ."

Hard words are full of potential. They can inform our spouse of how we truly think and feel. They can remove uncertainty. They allow our spouse to respond to who we truly are.

The way good couples keep an issue from turning personal is by using hard words, not harsh ones. What prevents most people from using hard words is fear. We are afraid that if we tell the truth, our words will be used against us. We will be attacked instead of protected. We will be manipulated rather than loved.

Oftentimes our fears have little to do with our spouse and much more to do with our upbringing or history. Maybe we've never seen constructive conversations take place. Without having a proper method modeled for us, we struggle to know how to fight. Maybe we have seen destructive conversations. Sometimes the only way a person knows how to fight is with personal attacks and hurtful words.

Yet if we can overcome our fears and find the courage to exchange harsh words for hard words, we can more easily find common ground on difficult issues.

Two Guardrails for Hard Conversations: Humility and Honesty

Communication is a key skill of good partnerships. When two people can clearly communicate about difficult topics, they can better understand one another and more easily find a workable plan of action.

Whenever hard conversations arise, every word spoken should stay between two guardrails: humility and honesty. These will keep the conversation out of the ditch and drive it toward an outcome.

Humility requires courage and trust. For many of us, humility goes against our normal way of approaching things. We need to humbly state our own opinion or frustration. Without pretense or anger, we can simply state the problem at hand.

As we communicate our point, we should also seek to understand our spouse with humility. We need to humbly ask our partner their opinion, idea, or concern. Many people come from backgrounds where nothing was asked directly, and now issues are hinted about or implied. We must reject passive aggressiveness and boldly confront issues.

Humility is expressed in three ways:

1. *In tone.* Humility is never harsh. It's never cutting. It has a softness and openness about it.
2. *In content.* Humility never assumes to know everything but seeks understanding.
3. *In attitude.* Humility is the antidote to contempt. We communicate with humility because we respect our spouse and believe they have something to say.

When we communicate this way, we are honoring the other person and recognizing their contribution to the relationship. This provides an opportunity for connection and understanding.

Honesty also requires courage and trust. When we reject honesty, we are choosing to hide and deceive. Without honesty, spouses give partial answers, tell half-truths, pretend nothing is wrong, or withhold feelings.

Choosing deceit is refusing to give our spouse our true selves. Either we fear rejection or we believe our spouse doesn't deserve the true us, but either way, deceit kills communication.

We owe it to ourselves and our spouse to communicate honestly. When we do so, we honor our spouse by showing them who we truly are. We indicate that we are fully engaged in the relationship and are willing to do whatever it takes to solve an issue. Honesty reminds us of a key truth about marriage—it is not our job to read our spouse's mind.

Couples often fall into the deception that love equates to mind reading. "If he really loved me, he wouldn't have to ask," she says. "If she would pay attention, she would know what I think," he says. Yet there may be no greater lie about marriage than the belief that married couples should be able to read each other's minds.

If you desire a spouse who can predict your every desire, know your every thought, and finish your every sentence, it is possible to experience that. If for fifty years of marriage you clearly communicate your thoughts and opinions, then maybe after a lifetime of living together your spouse will begin to understand what you think as the two of you are rocking away your final days at a nursing home.

But until then, it is the height of arrogance to think your spouse should be able to predict your thoughts. My wife can't predict my thoughts partly because half the time I don't even know what I'm thinking. My opinion changes. My attitudes shift. My desire is one thing one day and then completely different the next day. I can't expect her to know me when much of the time I don't even know myself.

I can't read her mind and she can't read mine. This leaves us with only one reasonable response—we will say what we mean. No games. No reading between the lines. No interpretation. I am responsible for saying what I mean, and my wife is responsible for taking me at my word.

Love is not the ability to know what our spouse is thinking without asking; love is taking the time to ask, listening, and acting in response to what our spouse tells us.

Because we can't read each other's minds, we must do the following:

Take each other's words at face value. If I say something, my wife must assume I mean it. I can't say one thing and expect her to interpret it as something else. If she says yes, she can't expect me to interpret it as, "I'm saying yes, but I really mean no, so you better not do it." Similarly, if I say I'm okay with something, I better be okay with it.

Assume we don't know what the other is thinking. Assumptions can be dangerous. If we assume we know what our spouse is thinking, we would be tempted not to ask them their thoughts. By assuming we don't know what they're thinking, we are more likely to communicate. If you are going to assume, assume you don't know.

Be understanding when we get it wrong. Marriage is supposed to be difficult. We are supposed to get it wrong sometimes. Being wrong allows us to grow. If we never made mistakes, we would never learn more about one another or ourselves. We would never truly need the love on which the relationship is based.

Everyone wants to be so connected with their spouse that they just know the other person. But getting to that point takes years of honesty, openness, and failure. If we are willing to put in the work, we might one day experience what we want.

Becoming that couple is not something that happens when we fall in love; it's a by-product of a lifetime of communication, shared experiences, and learning to understand one another.

The One Question That Determines Strong Partnership

An effective partnership is available to any couple if they will do the work to make it happen. It simply comes down to one question: are you willing to grow?

Any couple who is willing to grow can have an amazing partnership. No one is born a good partner. Being an effective husband or wife does not come naturally. While it might come easier to some, it is difficult for all. Those who become good husbands or wives do so because they are always learning, striving, and growing.

Any couple not willing to grow will never be the partner they should be. Marriage is not a static state. At every moment, each individual in the relationship is changing, the circumstances of life are changing, and what is necessary to be happily married is progressing. Unless a couple develops the ability to grow in positive ways, they will not be able to navigate marriage.

> *Unless a couple develops the ability to grow in positive ways, they will not be able to navigate marriage.*

Sadly, some individuals complain about a natural part of a healthy marriage. "She's changed," the husband says. "He's just not the same person," the wife says. They are often right in their description. The person they married is not the same person from five or ten years ago. But the problem is not that one spouse changed; the problem is that the other did not.

Change is a necessary aspect of marriage. Unless you are growing and adapting, your marriage is dying.

Healthy couples have the ability to learn and grow. Their greatest teacher is often conflict. Any relational rub is an opportunity to learn a new skill, grow in knowledge of one another, reveal their heart, and engineer a new element of the relationship.

Success is often viewed skeptically. While a healthy couple appreciates professional or personal success, they also have a deep awareness of the dangers of success. They work with great intention to find a deeper satisfaction with one another rather than allowing success to fill relationship voids.

Failure is viewed as an opportunity. Healthy couples see failure as a tremendous chance to explore mistakes and make better choices the next time. They do not blame one another but instead seek mutual understanding.

This growth mindset does not come naturally. People are not born this way; they make choices to become this way.

I can't speak into the specific issues of the failed marriages of Nelson Mandela, Henry Kissinger, Kofi Annan, Shimon Peres, and other Nobel Peace Prize winners, but their divorces don't surprise me. As difficult as international diplomacy is, marriage might be more difficult.

Yet I have a guess as to why some of these marriages failed. I would think it is very difficult for powerful men to have the humility to get help with their marriages. How does the leader of a country submit himself to a counselor, admitting he doesn't know how to be a good husband? How does a powerful negotiator seek help in finding common ground with his wife?

I could be wrong, but I imagine many of these men were great international leaders yet poor marital partners. They likely struggled because marriage consists of two equals. Manipulations, threats of force, or brilliant tactics do not work. As problems arose, they likely also struggled to seek help in the midst of their difficulty.

Whatever the reasons, the fact that famed negotiators have failed at marriage should both encourage us and warn us. We should be encouraged to know we are not alone in finding marriage difficult. The common frustrations we experience are likely experienced by everyone in marriage.

Yet we should also be warned. If professional negotiators struggle with marriage, what chance do we have? The answer is "very little," if we do not have the humility and desire required to do the work needed to become good partners.

BE INTENTIONAL

1. How is negotiation a positive aspect of a healthy marriage?
2. Are you able to discuss issues, or do you devolve into making things personal? How can you avoid the latter?

3. Which do you struggle with the most—taking your spouse's words at face value, assuming you don't know what they're thinking, or being understanding when you get it wrong? Why?

4. What prevents you from growing as a couple?

10

How to Make Her Dreams Come True

Partner doesn't have the beauty of the word *friend*. It lacks the sexiness of the word *lover*. It sounds cold and distanced. On the rare occasion in which a person thinks of the aspect of partnership within marriage, they consider it a necessary evil. To make life work, you have to be partners in order to be able to do what you want.

But partnership is far more than a necessary evil. For many couples it is a place with tremendous potential for growth. When a couple appreciates the possibilities of partnership and what it can do for their relationship, they can grow closer in ways they never thought possible.

Partnership is not just about work and parenting. Although those two aspects are very important, partnership is more than that. It's about creating the life you want.

We live in a fascinating time in which most readers of this book have more control over their lives than any generation before. The opportunities are not endless. There are still plenty of setbacks that prevent people from doing or being exactly what they want. However, the opportunities are plentiful. The average couple has tremendous freedom to choose the life they want to live.

Marriage should be a catalyst that propels us toward our dreams. One of the most fun aspects of marriage is waking up every day knowing someone else wants you to succeed. This should be a characteristic of every marriage. You should be your spouse's greatest cheerleader and they should be yours. If that element of the relationship is missing, something is wrong. We root for those we love. We cheer on those we have affection for.

Marriage should be a catalyst that propels us toward our dreams. One of the most fun aspects of marriage is waking up every day knowing someone else wants you to succeed.

In a healthy marriage, each person is doing everything in their power to make the other person's dreams come true. They are giving support and assistance for their spouse to experience what they have always hoped for.

Every year, Jenny and I take a vacation without the kids. Half the fun is choosing where to go and anticipating the trip. Jenny's favorite recreational activity is hiking, while I love to play golf, so we generally try to vacation in a spot where we can do both.

Recently, after putting the kids to bed, we both got on our laptops and started researching potential vacation spots. After a few minutes, Jenny asked me what I was researching and I said, "I'm looking at a list of the top national parks in the US. I figure I can find a good golf course nearby. What are you looking at?"

She laughed and said, "I'm looking at a list of the top ten golf courses in the US. I figure I can find a good national park nearby."

Whenever I think of who we want to be as partners, this episode comes to mind. This was us at our best (though there are plenty of other stories of us at our worst). At our best, neither of us denies what we want as individuals, and we try to make those things happen. But we seek what we desire as secondary to what our spouse wants.

This is marriage at its best—looking out for the interests of the other more than self, submitting our hopes and dreams to those of the other person even as they submit in return. When two people consistently—not perfectly but consistently—do that, the marriage can flourish.

It's when we begin to put ourselves above our spouse and use them as a tool for our own personal gain that marriage becomes destructive. In mutual submission, both partners are equal, but when the submission is one-sided, the relationship loses its equality. When my hopes trump the hopes of my wife, our relationship is out of balance.

Of course, there is a prerequisite for making this happen. In order to assist our spouse with their dreams or to gain assistance with our own dreams, we must have an intimate understanding of one another. We have to create a climate in which it is safe to truly risk communicating those hidden secrets and desires.

Many couples fail to be good partners in part because they never consider who they want to be either individually or together. They never define success.

A Prerequisite for Success

Who do you want to be? What do you want to accomplish? What legacy do you want to leave? These are questions that must be asked for a marriage partnership to be effective.

Consider the benefit of a budget. From a financial perspective, few things are as useful for most households as a budget. When couples go from haphazardly spending their money to consciously choosing what is important, they feel a sense of control over a previously uncontrollable situation. Without a budget, many households spend money without serious thought and often struggle paycheck to paycheck. With a budget, a family prioritizes what is important, puts their money where they want it to go, and begins to chip away at long-term goals.

As it is with money, so it is with marriage. Most couples do not define their hopes and dreams. They fail to describe success in a meaningful way, so they haphazardly make decisions in the moment rather than considering their long-term desires. They react to life rather than building a life.

Consider how little time most individuals or couples give to the following questions:

What does a successful marriage look like to you?

Who do you want to be as a husband/wife?

What are some skills you need to learn to become a better couple?

What are some personal goals you hope to achieve?

What are some goals you hope you and your spouse achieve?

What is something you hope to achieve over time?

What are some small steps you can take now to begin to achieve your goals?

Without discussing these questions, most couples are simply hoping they luck into success. Rather than building the life they want, they are reacting to the life given to them.

But it doesn't have to be this way. If a couple will work on a definition or description of success, they can begin to walk toward what they desire. Even if they can't define it, the very process of discussing success will make it more likely to happen.

Too many couples do not even know what success would look like if they experienced it. They assume it's more money or a bigger house or a better job title, never realizing that those things will not lead toward more life satisfaction but likely will further exploit weaknesses that exist in the marriage.

Without a picture of success, they don't even know what they are chasing.

Stop Spending Your Spouse's Dreams

If a couple has a clear understanding of what they want, an immediate practical change can take place. Without a clear direction of where they would like to go, they act in a haphazard way. Nowhere is this seen more than with finances.

Any couple who lives by a few basic financial principles can experience an easier marriage. If someone would save six months' worth of expenses, invest in retirement, give generously to others, and live off less than they make, then most fights regarding money would disappear.

Yet there is a connection that many couples fail to make when it comes to money and their dreams. Every dollar saved today can be a dollar spent tomorrow on a dream or on taking a risk. Yet every dollar foolishly spent today hinders our opportunities tomorrow.

Obviously we must spend money today. It's impossible to save every dollar we make. However, the sooner we learn to make wise choices regarding our finances, the greater our opportunities may be regarding what we hope to do and achieve.

When Jenny and I first got married, I met with a financial planner. It seemed like a pointless meeting since we didn't have any finances to plan for. However, the expert gave me some advice. Beyond providing a few basic principles, he urged us to save more than our peers, not for retirement (although he encouraged aggressive retirement savings) but for what he described as "opportunities you will experience a decade from now."

Having assisted many people with their finances, he knew that as a person matures into adulthood, families are established, and roots are put in place, opportunities will arise.

He was right. We saved extra money in an account that was neither for retirement nor for any other known expense. It was for unknown opportunities.

Sure enough, about a decade after we married, opportunities began to present themselves—friends were starting businesses and looking for investors, popular stocks hit all-time lows, a piece of investment property was for sale.

We couldn't do everything, but we did have the option of doing some things. Eventually an opportunity presented itself that we had never considered. Jenny had been very successful in her career, but she was burning out. She considered quitting when one day the thought hit her: *Why not start my own company?* She is a worker by nature, so she knew she would do something. Why not do something where we would more fully reap the benefits?

We took our time and made our plans, and Jenny started her own company. We had no idea how long it would take to get off the ground, or even if it *could* get off the ground. Yet because we had saved money, there was no pressure. We had enough money saved that she could take two years to establish the company without it negatively impacting our daily lives.

Because we saved, Jenny was able to accomplish a dream she didn't even have when we began saving.

Whenever we fail to live by good financial principles, we are doing more than just straining our relationships; we are also suffocating our dreams. For many, even if the perfect opportunity presented itself, they would not be able to take advantage of it because they could not go two weeks without a paycheck, much less two years.

> *Whenever we fail to live by good financial principles, we are doing more than just straining our relationships; we are also suffocating our dreams.*

Sadly, foolish decisions shackle us later in life. Bad decisions today can close the doors of opportunity tomorrow.

Interestingly, whenever we see saving money as an investment in our dreams, it is easier to do. But when we lose the connection between saving today and dreaming tomorrow, it becomes much more tempting to make poor choices today.

Healthy couples have an ability to delay gratification. Unhealthy couples do not. As their marriage suffers, the temptation grows to find any type of satisfaction today. Commonly, the result is poor decision making regarding finances.

Unfortunately, when we seek happiness today at the expense of happiness tomorrow, we often end up with it neither today nor tomorrow. But when we are satisfied enough in our relationship today, we can make sacrifices in order to experience success tomorrow. Then we often find happiness both today and tomorrow.

Partnership and Money

When most people hear the word *partnership*, they quickly associate it with money. And rightfully so. How a couple handles their finances will play a big role in their satisfaction with their marriage. However, it plays a different role in marriage than most people think.

Nearly every survey shows the number one source of conflict for married couples is money. Yet no marriage truly ends because of money. Money is never the disease; it is always the symptom.

When I was in college, a friend broke up with his longtime girlfriend. The breakup surprised me, so I asked my friend about it. He said, "She wants to be a doctor. I can't marry someone who is going to make more money than me."

I laughed and said, "Can I have her number?"

While a man is free to date or not to date whomever he wishes for whatever reasons he wishes, I found my friend's thinking to be a little foolish. In a partnership, both spouses contribute equally to the success of the marriage. One might bring in a larger salary than the other. One may not even receive an official salary, but both contribute to the success of the relationship. The equality of the couple is not determined by salary. It is determined by their equal work, passion, and contribution.

Healthy couples always talk about money in a similar way. They discuss "our money." Whether in power couples where both spouses have six-figure incomes, or in traditional families where the husband works outside the home and the wife works in the home, the philosophy is the same: "We are a team, and we own everything equally."

The equality of the couple is not determined by salary. It is determined by their equal work, passion, and contribution.

In a true partnership, it doesn't matter who makes the most money. The money belongs to both spouses as each contributes to the success of the whole. How money is spent is also agreed on by both partners. They might experience moments of disagreement. They might have to regularly negotiate some expenses. They might even have to seek an outside advisor to help determine the best course of action, but they do find a working agreement on how much to spend, where to spend it, and what priorities take precedence.

If you ask Wendy, she and her husband divorced because of money. They never could agree on it. Both she and Devin assumed if they just made more money, most of their problems would go away. Yet every time one of them received a raise, the money seemed to disappear.

They constantly fought about the issue. Devin said Wendy was irresponsible and selfish. She couldn't control her shopping, and the credit card bills piled up. Wendy thought Devin was a hypocrite. Sure, he would go months without spending a dime, but with one quarterly purchase, he would spend more than she had in all those months.

The fights began to influence every aspect of their relationship, and eventually they'd had enough. Anytime Wendy reads a survey about marital problems, she isn't surprised that money tops the list.

Actually, Wendy and Devin are wrong. They divorced for several reasons, but none of them were about money:

Lack of communication. They never learned how to properly communicate about money. Every discussion got personal quickly. They could not understand each other and why money was a struggle.

Apathy. Neither read a finance book. They never went to a financial planner or reached out to a mentor couple. They never took a class together to learn about personal finance.

Selfishness. Both assumed the other person was the problem. They each believed they deserved to spend the money they were spending, but the other spouse should have to cut back their expenses because of the couple's debt. When one spouse is unable to submit their desire to what is best for the marriage, it will often be revealed in how they spend their money.

Addiction. Wendy and Devin were both addicted to spending. It expressed itself in different ways—Wendy with near daily purchases and Devin with occasional large purchases—but it was the same issue. In response to a poor marriage and the loneliness it created, both partners found meaning in money. They coped with their stress by spending, and their poor coping created more stress.

Money was the symptom. Both Wendy and Devin saw it, but what neither saw were the underlying diseases that ultimately destroyed their relationship. People do not get divorced because of money, but it is regularly the symptom they notice in a bad relationship. Money reveals our hearts, and a couple who constantly argues over money has a problem at the heart of their relationship.

An Example of Partnership: When Dad Works and Mom Stays Home

Whenever I speak about partnership with couples, a common question arises. While the question doesn't apply to everyone, the principle behind it is applicable to every couple. Partnership is clearly one of the cornerstones of a healthy marriage. When both spouses feel as though they are not alone in this life but are jointly pursuing similar goals and aspirations, their marriage can flourish.

Inevitably when considering these ideas, a man will ask, "How do we feel a sense of partnership when I work and my wife stays home?" Many women do not love this question, but I do, because it allows me to make a very important point regarding money, partnership, and the core concepts of what marriage is all about.

The question itself shows biases that hinder the couple from experiencing the true benefits of partnership. It unearths two assumptions that create tension in marriage, both of which are tragically wrong.

The first assumption is that when one spouse receives a paycheck for their job and the other does not, then only one spouse is earning money.

For a married couple, money is never "hers" and "his." One or both spouses might receive a check with their name on it. Separate checking accounts might be kept because it's the best financial plan for the couple. But all the money belongs to both spouses because all the money is earned by both spouses.

I have a job outside the home. Twice a month I receive a paycheck with my name on it. But I can't do my job without my wife. I do only half of the chauffeuring around of our kids (and actually less than half because of my mom's help). I do only some of the housework. There are some specific places where I take the lead responsibility to run our house. In order to free myself to work, I do only some of the things at home.

The same is true for Jenny. She doesn't take the kids to school or run them to every extracurricular activity or do every aspect of housework. She does a lot, but she doesn't do it all. She can't, because she needs time to do her job.

There are times when I am taking care of our private lives so Jenny can take care of her business. At the same time, Jenny is taking care of other aspects of our private lives so I can do my job. Without the other person we would still do our jobs, but many changes would have to take place.

The life we have together, we have built together. No matter who makes more money or less money or no money, every dollar earned by one of us is a dollar earned by both of us.

This is true for every couple. When Dad works and Mom stays home, Mom is playing a key role in the money Dad earns. The paycheck might be in his name, but it is their money. He has no right to assume he is making all of the money. Together they have designed a life based on one paycheck, but they jointly share the responsibilities to make that life happen.

This is why the courts rightly split the possessions 50/50 when a divorce occurs. The man doesn't deserve more just because he went to work.

One of the first steps to experiencing true partnership with your spouse if one of you stays home and the other works outside the home is to recognize the contribution the other person is making toward what you do. If a husband's paycheck allows the wife to stay home, she should recognize with gratitude the opportunity he gives her. If a wife works from home while her husband goes to work, he should recognize with gratitude the opportunity she gives him.

The second assumption the above question reveals regarding partnership is that it is primarily about money. It is not. Money is important, but it is not the main aspect of partnership. Partnership is about life. It is about creating the life we desire. Money plays only a secondary role in that life.

Husbands and wives are life partners. Partnership should define every aspect of our lives. It's about money and work, but it is also about parenting, family, fun, hobbies, dreams, aspirations, our home, a spiritual connection, and every other pursuit.

Even if one spouse has nothing to do with how the other spouse earns money (which is impossible), they should still feel a deep sense of partnership in multiple areas of life.

Couples parent as partners. Parenting should never be left to one parent. It is a team sport. While there might be specific roles that each person plays, there is no single issue regarding children in which both parents aren't involved. Children should know and feel that their parents are partners. As they try to divide their parents (and they will), parents should work hard to keep the partnership intact. Not only does it make the parents feel stronger, it gives the children a greater sense of security.

Couples dream as partners. Part of a spouse's job is to help their husband or wife experience some of their lifelong goals. Many things cannot be accomplished alone. We need help. A spouse can be a constant source of encouragement, hope, and prodding. We can refuse to let our spouse give up on themselves or on those things that are important to them. We can confront them when we feel as though they are settling for less than what is possible.

Couples play as partners. It is not important for spouses to share every hobby. It is actually beneficial if there are some things a husband or wife does without their spouse. But it is useful for couples to share some hobbies. Too many marriages get stuck in the routine of work and raising kids, and couples lose the element of fun in their relationship. Having a shared hobby can invigorate a relationship.

The Heart of Partnership

One of the greatest privileges of marriage is to wake up every morning and know that at least one other person cares about my life as much as I do. They are seeking my best as passionately as I am. It is a wonderful gift to be able to reciprocate my wife's fervor for me with my own fervor for her.

This is the heart of partnership—two people fully committed to the well-being and success of their spouse. As they each benefit the other, they receive benefits from the relationship. Each individual thrives as the relationship itself thrives.

As often as possible, I try to ask Jenny, "What's one way I can help you today?" Whether you have been married one day or seventy years, this question can strengthen your partnership and help your relationship.

BE INTENTIONAL

1. What are your spouse's dreams? How are you helping them come true?
2. Take time to discuss the questions on page 140.
3. Is there any place in your life in which you feel like it is all "me" and not "us"?
4. What is one way you can help your partner today?

PART 3

LOVER

11

The Appeal of Easy Sex

Of the three elements of a healthy marriage—friend, partner, and lover—friendship is the most important. Everything flows from it. But the unique aspect of a marriage is the intimate relationship between husband and wife.

In the best of scenarios, a healthy couple will have many meaningful friendships. They will be partners with a variety of people. But they should have physical intimacy with only one person. Sex is a unique connection meant for husband and wife.

Being lovers is about more than just sex. It is an erotic dance happening between two people that intertwines with every aspect of their relationship. Sex is the key element of the dance, but it isn't the only one.

Intimacy between two people adds a critical third element to a marriage. Friendship is two people walking hand in hand, side by side, through life. As friends, you always know someone is by your side. Partnership is two people living life back-to-back, always scanning the horizon for potential threats or opportunities. As partners, you always know someone has your back. Lovers are two people standing face-to-face, looking each other in the eye. As lovers, you always know someone sees you and loves you.

The intimate side of a marriage relationship can be a deeply meaningful aspect of life. Feeling cherished, valued, desired, and loved can assist a person in becoming fully alive. Yet because of shame, guilt, insecurity, and the evil potential of humanity, this aspect of marriage is fraught with peril.

Whenever I speak with couples before their wedding, I try to get an idea of what their expectations are for the relationship. Expectations often determine outcomes. With the right expectations, a couple can navigate the marital relationship with great success. With the wrong ones, even the best of relationships will struggle.

A Misconception about Married Sex

The biggest misconception young couples have of marriage is that sex will be easy. We want sex to be easy. We assume it should be so. Attraction is easy. As soon as hormones kick in, a child begins their journey to adulthood, and it is no struggle to be attracted to someone. It's exciting and enjoyable.

> *The biggest misconception young couples have of marriage is that sex will be easy.*

The culmination of attraction is a sexual encounter, and we assume that something that begins without effort will continue without effort. Yet nothing could be further from the truth. Great sex is rarely easy.

It might begin easily. For most, the sexual relationship in the first year of marriage is not difficult. It happens frequently and without much complication. But give it some time. Add children. Expand work responsibilities. Go through a few arguments. Hold a few grudges. Watch your vulnerability be tried and then questioned, and your expectations unmet.

Sex becomes difficult.

It feels as though it shouldn't be that way. Many years ago I lay in bed and told my wife that I understood the appeal of prostitution. She nervously laughed and said, "Oh really?"

I replied, "You've served people all day long. You worked all day to help others with what they needed. You came home, cooked dinner, played with the kids, and served our family. I've done the same. All day long I was giving of myself to help other people. Now, fourteen hours after we got up, the day is almost done and we are trying to have sex. How nice would it be not to have to give anymore and simply be served?"

She agreed. This is the appeal of sex in the movies. When we find sex far too complicated, we assume we are missing the key that will make it easy. At this point, ease is often offered in two ways—find someone who will do whatever I want and is solely about my pleasure, or submit myself to someone else so I don't have to make any decisions.

Either way, that's sex without the constraints of a mutually respectful and caring relationship. It removes the give-and-take dance of healthy sexuality. Either it exploits our pride and allows us to demean others, or it manipulates our insecurities and allows us to be used by others. Neither is the true intent of sex.

Sex is supposed to be an erotic interaction between two equals. It is the place where we can both be vulnerable and gain strength from each other. It is one area that on occasion can make us feel most alive, most like a man or a woman, and most connected with the person we love.

But it won't every time. In fiction, sex appears easy, but real sex is much messier than we like it to be. It confronts our deepest insecurities and wounds. It tempts us with an easy love, only to leave us with complexity and difficulty. It lures us to trust but then causes us to question. It gives amplification to the voices in our heads saying, "You are not loveable" or "You are not worthy" or "Something is wrong with you."

Sex in real life is so complex and personal that we often trade meaningful sex for a mirage. Pornography and prostitution promise sex without emotional demands, and sex outside of marriage promises the physical experience without any responsibilities. But they are all a mirage of the real thing. They never fully provide what they promise.

Sex in real life is so complex and personal that we often trade meaningful sex for a mirage.

I understand the appeal of easy sex. Life is difficult enough—shouldn't something be easy? Maybe, but sex isn't that something. It challenges us and tests our relationship. Because it is one of the best things about marriage, it is also one of the more frustrating elements.

Resist the temptation toward easy sex. Have the courage and wisdom to know real sex is more complicated than what you read in fiction. But it's worth it.

The Key to Married Sex

Because sex is complicated, difficult, and emotionally charged, it is vital that a couple develop the ability to talk about the subject in a safe, caring, open, and productive way. A couple who can have a good conversation about sex can develop a healthy sex life. A couple who cannot safely discuss it might have occasionally good sex, but rarely will they develop a healthy sex life. Too many things will be left unsaid—likes, desires, dislikes, and fears. When a couple cannot discuss sex without feeling ashamed, guilty, insecure, attacked, or unheard, they are unlikely to have their own needs met or to meet the other person's needs.

And yet we do talk about sex. We are quick to communicate about the topic over lunch, in locker rooms, or at the office. We will talk to our friends, but not our spouse.

Couples who fail to communicate well about sex usually hold one of three mindsets:

1. *Good sex should happen naturally.* There is no need to talk since everyone knows how to have sex. If sex isn't going well for a couple, they assume the problem is their spouse, not their lack of communication.
2. *Good people don't discuss sex.* Believing sex is bad and dirty, they get embarrassed to talk about the act.
3. *Talking about sex isn't worth the risk of rejection.* When a discussion about sex doesn't go well, the temptation is not to broach the topic again. If a conversation goes poorly, it can result in a fight or in feelings of deep hurt.

The answer to these three mindsets is humility, truth, and mercy. These elements that characterize a good partnership now enhance our intimacy. Humility recognizes that we don't know everything and we all need to learn. Truth recognizes that sex is an important part of every good marriage, but because of the frailty of humanity, we will all struggle with certain aspects of it. Every couple will have to work through sexual problems—that's part of being married. Mercy gives us extreme patience and kindness with ourselves and our spouse when discussing difficult topics.

With humility, truth, and mercy, couples can learn how to talk to one another about sex. This is never just one conversation; it is ongoing through the life of your marriage, including discussions about insecurities, expectations, turn-ons, turnoffs, fears, and fantasies. It's only by discussing these topics that we can learn how to bring pleasure to one another.

Yet there is one time that couples should not talk about sex. A good conversation about it should happen over dinner or on a walk or just before sex or well after sex, but it should not happen at the time or place you normally have sex.

While it's okay to give helpful suggestions during sex ("yes," "no," "more," "here," etc.), it is not productive to have an in-depth discussion during sex. Conversations about the topic can be difficult. They need to happen in the safety of a loving relationship and outside the atmosphere of expectation.

Consider a pair of ice dancers or a Hall of Fame quarterback and his best wide receiver. Both partners experience success only to the level that they can communicate about a game plan and be open with one another about what is happening. They read one another's body language and might give a brief command, but they don't talk when they are performing. They talk before and after, but not during. As it is with ice dancers and football players, so it should be with couples. Talk about sex in practice, but don't talk about it during the game.

Healthy couples talk about sex. There is nothing off-limits when it comes to conversation. Unhealthy couples don't talk about it. They are overconfident, afraid, or gun-shy.

The best way for a couple to improve their sex life is to have an ongoing conversation. When was the last time you had a meaningful discussion with your spouse about sex? How about now?

Stereotypes and Generalizations

I'm often hesitant to write or speak about sex because I do so in generalities, always aware there are specific situations in which my words may not apply. They are proverbial truth, not absolute law.

In most relationships, a man has a higher sex drive than a woman. Often the statistic of 70 percent is given. So in most marriages, the guy wants more sex than the woman. Whenever I write about sex, I often keep that generalization in mind. But I'm very aware that even as I encourage women to have more sex with their husbands, some women who would love for that to happen are in the 30 percent group who have a higher sex drive than their husband. It's the husband who needs to heed the advice, not the wife.

In other scenarios, a wife might be in an abusive relationship, read my advice, and feel guilt for not wanting to sleep with her husband. While I would never tell her to have sex with someone who abuses her, because I write with generalizations in mind, the words can be confused.

Like all words, but especially when they are about sex, these chapters need to be read with serious discernment. I'm writing to a generally healthy couple who could use a little advice for improvement. If there is a history of sexual abuse or a present addiction or some other factors that set your relationship outside the general norm, read the following pages with discernment. Never use them to guilt your spouse or to demand some action. Be fair in looking at your own actions in comparison with the general truths we will cover. Because these are important issues, never hesitate to seek help from a professional counselor.

If I Could Tell Wives One Thing

Wives, you can spend the rest of your marriage trying to understand the importance of sex in the lives of men, especially your husband, but you will never fully get it. Even your husband can't completely explain it. He likely views sex in a different way than you. He is not wrong, and neither are you. For a healthy sex life to develop, start by realizing it's okay to feel differently than your husband about sex.

For a healthy sex life to develop, start by realizing it's okay to feel differently than your husband about sex.

One of the questions I frequently receive from women is, "Is my husband a pervert?" My answer is always, "Well, that depends." On some occasions, the answer is yes. Because of pornography, past abuse, or some other factor, the husband desires sexual activity that should be considered out-of-bounds. He wants to add another person or treat his spouse in a demeaning way, and that is a perversion of what sex is meant to be.

But in most situations, the answer is no. The husband simply views sex differently than his wife. If he has a natural desire for sex and his wife defines that as a perversion, it will not only be a hindrance to their sex life, but it will also attack his identity.

I've sat with many couples and heard the wife call her husband a pervert, so I ask why she labels him that way. While I agree with some women when I hear more of the story, many times I simply shake my head and say, "He is not a pervert; he is a man, and that is how a man views sex."

A man's desire for sex is healthy, and it can greatly enhance the marriage for both partners when it is appreciated and allowed to be properly expressed.

If I could tell wives one thing in regard to marriage, it would be to continually grow in appreciating the power of sex to the male mind, especially their husbands.

Sex is powerful. So powerful it will damage a relationship before marriage. As I often tell single women, do not sleep with a man until he is willing to die for you. When men engage in premarital sex, they cannot think clearly enough to make the best decision regarding marriage. Sex is so powerful it clouds their ability to make a rational decision. When sex is present before marriage, some men delay marriage because they are already getting some of the privileges of being married without any of the responsibility. Other men get married but lose their sense of discernment because sex causes them to minimize other differences.

Men often feel intimacy through sex. While many women have sex as a result of intimacy, many men feel intimacy because of sex. Every time you hear your husband talk about sex, realize he is also talking about intimacy, though it may not be intimacy the way you think of it (and remember, neither viewpoint is better than the other). This small switch in thinking can greatly change many marriages. "All he wants is sex," I often hear. "All he wants is you," I often tell women in reply. "That is a compliment, and you should take it as such."

When you reject sex, your husband feels like you are rejecting him. I'm not saying you are. I'm not saying this is right. I am simply saying how it most often feels to him. To reject sex feels impersonal to you but feels very personal to a man. Yet you should still have a right to reject it. This is one reason I created the twenty-four-hour rule. It gives the wife the ability to reject sex but gives the husband a set time frame within which sex will occur. "Not now" is given a time limit. I've yet to meet a man who dislikes the twenty-four-hour rule. (For more on this rule, see chapter 14.)

To the extent you make sex a priority, your husband will feel like you have made him a priority. On a regular basis, I meet women who claim their family is a top priority, but somehow their husband will not feel like part of that.

We do not have the right to tell our spouse what they can and cannot care about. Even if you don't understand the sexual needs of your spouse, you still care about him. If he cares about it, you should too.

You are your husband's only proper sexual outlet. This should be his boundary and your encouragement. When a man says "I do" to you, he is saying "I won't" to every other woman on the planet. He needs to live by his vow. But you can recognize the magnitude of what he has promised. This doesn't mean you should feel pressure to do everything he desires, but it should give you a great sense of responsibility for creating a regular opportunity for sex.

Sex is not everything. It's not even the most important thing. Yet it is a vital component to a healthy marriage. When a wife ignores it, her husband feels ignored. When she makes an intentional effort to accept her husband's viewpoint of sex, he feels heard, understood, and desired.

If I Could Tell Husbands One Thing

Many years into marriage, I was having a conversation with Jenny when I said, "Wives have it easy."

She laughed and said, "How so?"

"Generally speaking, for a man to be happy, his wife only needs to focus on one thing. If that is right, most everything else will be right. I just wish there was one thing I could consistently do to make you happy."

She gave me a serious look and said, "There is. Clean the kitchen." For my wife, cleaning the kitchen is an act of service. When I serve her (and the family), she feels valued, supported, and a part of a team. This makes her heart come alive. When I fail to serve her, she feels used, isolated, and overlooked. This makes her heart die.

Nearly every couple who comes to me after the wife has had an affair has one thing in common—her heart slowly died. Men tend to have affairs for a variety of reasons, and many men have affairs in spite of having a good marriage. But if a woman has an affair, in nearly every case it is because her heart has slowly died. The affair happens at the end of the process, not the beginning.

If I could tell husbands one thing, it would be that they have a responsibility to engage the heart of their wife. What are her hopes? What are her lifelong dreams? What makes her feel valued? What words mean the most to her? What are the small actions that she values the most? What are the day-to-day chores that are wearing her out?

Husbands do not naturally understand the hearts of their wives. There is no way for us to. In the same way that women cannot naturally know their husbands, husbands cannot naturally know their wives. It takes communication, a willingness to share our true feelings, and trial and error.

This is the great pursuit of marriage: learning what our spouse's deepest needs and desires are and trying to do our part to fulfill them. Ultimately a wife is in charge of her own heart, but she deserves a partner who will help her keep it fully alive. When a woman's heart is fully alive, there is nothing in this world more beautiful.

For most women, sex is part of a larger pattern of feeling loved and valued, not a prerequisite. So when a marriage is working well, one partner needs sex to feel valued, and the other partner has sex when they feel valued. Both appreciate the differing perspective of their spouse and do everything in their power to meet the other's needs. The man does not wait to honor, value, and serve his wife until he is sexually satisfied. He is diligent in understanding her needs even before his are met. At the same time, the woman does not wait to have sex until after she feels recognized and served. She seeks to meet her husband's needs even before her own are met.

> *When a marriage is working well, one partner needs sex to feel valued, and the other partner has sex when they feel valued.*

In this scenario, both spouses will feel loved, honored, and respected most of the time. They will also have more sex, both because he desires it and because the conditions will be right for her desire to grow. It is a situation that builds off their differences.

However, when a relationship is in an unhealthy spot, instead of the differences helping the marriage, they hinder it. The man refuses to do anything until his needs are met. The woman feels less attracted to sex because of his selfishness and refuses to meet his needs until she feels more valued and served. She therefore has sex with him less often, making him less likely to do the things she needs. The relationship can quickly become toxic.

Most relationships will have moments in which both of these scenarios happen. In an unhealthy relationship, the couple will never recognize the dynamic at work or do anything to change the climate. In a healthy relationship, they spend far more time in the first scenario, and when they digress into the second, one or both spouses recognize what is happening and stop it. They begin to serve one another, and the relationship returns back to where it is supposed to be.

Husbands and wives view sex differently, but that's not the cause of frustration regarding sex. Frustration and fights are the result of couples either not being aware of the differences or refusing to appreciate how their spouse's views about sex are different from their own.

BE INTENTIONAL

1. Why do we assume sex should be easy? How do these assumptions hurt our intimacy?

2. Can you and your spouse freely discuss sexual issues without shame or fear? What role does good communication play in a healthy sex life?

3. How does your viewpoint of sex differ from that of your spouse? Is one right and the other wrong, or do you simply have different perspectives?

4. How can you leverage your differences to become strengths?

12

Three Types of Married Sex

In marriage, sex generally falls into one of three main types, and each type serves a different purpose and plays an important role in nourishing a well-rounded sex life.

The first type is spontaneous sex. When people think of sex, this is what most often comes to mind. It's the type of sex that just happens. A couple is attracted to one another both physically and emotionally. The energy builds and leads to an experience of unplanned passion. It's fun, natural, and an important part of any marriage.

Spontaneous sex is easy in the early years. During the honeymoon phase, it might be the only sex necessary. But as kids come along and the stresses of life increase, spontaneity can decrease. After being married for just a short time, a married couple must add the other two types of sex. At the same time, the longer a couple has been married, the more important it is for them to continue to include spontaneous rendezvous in their sexual diet.

When spontaneous sex dies, a couple can quickly fall into a marital rut. Spontaneity is vital so that sex doesn't become predictable and boring.

The second type of sex is scheduled sex. Planning sex sounds like a turnoff to many people. When I talk to a couple considering marriage, they often wrinkle their noses at the mention of scheduled sex. They can't imagine it being necessary or useful. I ask them, "Do you plan on having sex on your honeymoon?" Of course they do. They are already scheduling it.

The misconception about scheduled sex is that it won't be any good. It might be acceptable, but it is not as good as spontaneous sex. This isn't true. Scheduling Thanksgiving dinner does not make the dinner second rate. Planning a vacation doesn't hurt the experience of the vacation. As a matter of fact, half the fun of planning important things is the anticipation that goes into them. Imagine if the Super Bowl just suddenly happened. It wouldn't be nearly as good without the two weeks of pregame hype and preparations. Most important things in life are planned. It only makes sense for sex to be one of those things.

Scheduled sex becomes more important when the partnership between husband and wife fully develops. As the couple is raising kids, working on careers, and caught in a busy season of life, scheduling sex becomes necessary. As hectic as life can become, planning time to be alone is vital for the relationship. If you've never tried to schedule sex with your spouse, try it and see if it's as boring as people think. I've yet to meet a couple who practices scheduled sex and says it is boring.

By scheduling sex, a couple can make sure the spouse with a higher sex drive is better satisfied and is not left wondering when the next event might occur. It also gives both spouses the opportunity to reject a sexual encounter if they do not feel well or aren't in the mood, while still giving the other spouse hope of when the next encounter will occur. Every couple schedules sex—honeymoon, anniversaries, birthdays, certain holidays. Wise couples simply schedule it more often.

The third type of sex is often the most overlooked, but it is still equally necessary. It is maintenance sex. Because in nearly every relationship one partner has a higher drive than the other, some compromise will have to take place regarding the frequency of sex. If a couple only has as much sex as the lower-drive spouse desires, they will not have a healthy sex life. It must be more than the lowest desired, but it will probably be less than what the higher-drive spouse wants.

A wise couple discusses frequency on a regular basis and negotiates a general agreement of how often sex will occur. It should never be a concrete number per week, but it should be a working agreement. For this to happen, some sex will have to be maintenance sex. This is an encounter primarily for the higher-drive partner.

This might take some effort from the lower-drive partner, but it is worth it. One mistake many couples make is to think the higher-drive partner is wrong for wanting more sex. This isn't true. Many times I see couples in which one partner claims the other "wants too much sex," and when I ask how much is too much, the amount stated is a very normal amount. A high sex drive is not wrong. Our drives are different, and compromise should determine how often we have sex.

The concept of maintenance sex is related to an important topic regarding marital sex. It is not necessary for both partners to orgasm every time for a sexual encounter to be successful. Maybe one wants sex and the other doesn't. Maybe one partner is too tired but enjoys the closeness of the encounter. Maybe the female orgasm is so intense that she doesn't need it to feel satisfied each time. Many women say an orgasm isn't necessary with each encounter. Ironically, it is more men than women who believe women have to orgasm every time or the experience isn't productive. This simply isn't true.

While couples must be careful to make sure the whole concept of sex doesn't become one-sided (e.g., sex is just for him), it is perfectly acceptable for a single encounter to be one-sided. And even if it isn't, a woman does not always need to orgasm to have a good experience. In most relationships, a man will orgasm every time, but a woman won't. That is perfectly acceptable. As long as the woman is satisfied with the couple's sex life, she has every right to opt out of an orgasm. Of course, if she desires to climax, her husband should do what is necessary to assist her.

Are You Having Enough Sex?

The question many couples ask regarding sex is, "Are we having enough?" It's a common question, but it isn't the best question. A better question would be, "How do we develop a deep sense of satisfaction with our sex life," or, "How can we have more sex?" These two questions seek flourishing rather than minimums. They pursue a desired outcome rather than attempting to fulfill the bare minimum.

Yet to answer the common question, here is a simple test: Imagine you've scheduled sex. Maybe it's a birthday, an anniversary, Valentine's Day, or just an agreed-upon rendezvous. No matter the scenario, you both plan on having sex tonight. Because of that, the whole day is different. It's filled with flirting. Moods are elevated. Communication is enhanced.

After work, the babysitter arrives. You choose a nice restaurant. The night goes perfectly. When you return home, the babysitter leaves, the kids are put to bed, and the time has arrived. But there's an issue. Maybe you ate too much. Maybe the night went too late. Maybe what began as a scratchy throat has given way to a cold. Maybe work calls. Whatever the issue, what was supposed to be the highlight of the night doesn't take place. What happens?

Disappointment and frustration are understandable. But is there trust? Compassion? Understanding? Or is there anger? Bitterness?

Deep division? Extreme hurt or anger following this scenario can be a symptom of several issues, but the most obvious may be the frequency, or infrequency, of sex. The more satisfied a couple is with sexual frequency, the less influence one episode has on their feelings as a couple. If one disappointment causes an extreme response, the problem is something other than that event.

Consider it this way: The longer it's been since your last meal, the more important your next meal will be. If you skipped breakfast this morning, you would probably be pretty frustrated if you had to work through lunch. Yet if you had a late breakfast and ate more than normal, you may not even be upset if your lunch meeting cancels.

If your spouse gets a headache tonight and doesn't desire sex, will it be a minor frustration or a major fight? If it's the former, you are probably having enough sex. If it's the latter, you probably need to consider increasing the frequency.

There is something else to consider on this issue. Junk food is far more tempting when we are hungry. It's much easier to make wise choices regarding food when our stomachs are satisfied. The same is true with sex. While an individual is responsible for their own decisions and adultery is clearly forbidden, a husband or wife can assist their

> *The more satisfied a couple is with sexual frequency, the less influence one episode has on their feelings as a couple.*

spouse by making sure they are satisfied with their sex lives. To regularly starve our spouse and then send them out in a junk-food world is foolishness.

Your spouse was created to desire sex. It is an activity meant to be shared only between a husband and wife. If your spouse desires sex and you are the only appropriate sexual outlet they have, this should influence your perspective on frequency in sex. Knowing your spouse is going to face a lot of "junk food" tomorrow, what do you plan to cook for them tonight?

I Wouldn't Sleep with You Either

While frequency in sex is important and sex is a fair expectation within marriage, a spouse must be careful not to feel entitled to sex even when they are failing to live up to the other parts of marriage: friendship and partnership.

I was having lunch one day in a male-dominated restaurant. While I was trying to pay attention to the conversation at my table, I couldn't help but overhear the people at the table next to us. One of the men was railing against his wife: "She never does this. She never does that. She's always on me."

Then he said, "I played golf yesterday and then stayed in the clubhouse to watch the game. When I got home at 10:30, my wife just huffed at me and went to bed." He was complaining that they hadn't had sex.

As I listened to the rant, one thought kept occurring: *I wouldn't sleep with you either.* This man felt a great injustice. While there might be more to the story, based only on the information I heard, what gives him the right to expect sex? Yes, she is his wife, but what had he done as her husband? He spent the day playing golf with friends. He left her home alone. After his game, he didn't go home, take her to dinner, find out how her day had gone. Instead, he stayed late, avoided home, and spent more time with his friends. When he finally did go home, he was late, she was hurt, and he couldn't believe she didn't want to have sex.

It was almost comical to hear. Imagine if the man had asked her out for their first date on a Friday night. He then ignored her all day Friday, skipped dinner with her so he could be with his friends, and at the very end of the evening showed up on her doorstep for a good-night kiss. Clearly it wouldn't happen.

Instead, the man likely put serious time and thought into planning out the best evening possible, dressed up, picked her up, spent ample time with her, and over six months to a year, did everything in his power to woo her heart.

She had far more of a right to wonder why he stopped trying to woo her than he had a right to question why she wouldn't sleep with him after the game.

In marriage, we often wrongly assume our spouse will continue doing the things we like even if we stop doing the things they like. It is a form of entitlement. Instead of seeing the marriage relationship as a give-and-take of mutual benefit, we begin to believe we are entitled to all the privileges of marriage even if we fail to carry out its responsibilities.

Imagine if every interaction you have with your spouse today was the first set of interactions you ever had with them. Would she give you her phone number? Would he call you? Based on how you acted today, would he ask you to marry him? Would she say yes?

One of the most foolish decisions a couple makes is the choice to stop pursuing their spouse with the intensity and purpose with which they began the relationship. Clearly life changes and we don't have to do exactly what we did when we were dating, but the basic effort required on a first date is still required in the fifteenth year of marriage. We still must pursue one another.

I took the kids to play Putt-Putt once. As we played, there were three teenage couples also playing. It was funny to watch them. The boys were trying hard. They were laughing loudly, acting goofy, and doing everything in their power to impress their dates. At what point do men stop doing this? When do we no longer attempt to earn the attention of our woman? When does hope turn to entitlement? When does effort turn to expectation?

I'm sure this is not a one-way street. At what point do women stop trying? Every girl at the park was dressed nicely and was joking with her date, and for goodness' sake, they were playing Putt-Putt. I seriously doubt that game was the main focus for those girls when the boys asked them out. Few things are more boy-centered than Putt-Putt. Yet there they were.

But where are you? Men, are you pursuing your wife? Are you working to get her attention, to impress her, to make her laugh, to love her, to support her, to be her man? Women, are you pursuing your husband? Are you laughing at his silliness, taking time out of your busyness to do something with him, working to get your husband's look, attention, and affection?

We are foolish if we think we can hold strong affections for one another without any effort.

We are foolish if we think we can hold strong affections for one another without any effort. Love must be kindled or it will die. We either work at it with great intention or we lose it in unconscious apathy. If you aren't trying, you are dying.

When you think about sexual frequency in marriage, consider your attitude, your effort, and how hard you are working at pursuing your spouse's heart. Then ask yourself, "Would *I* sleep with me?"

What I Tell College Students about Married Sex

On occasion I teach communications classes at a local university. It's fun to be in a classroom with twenty-five twenty-year-olds who are being forced to take introduction to public speaking.

When teaching the importance of having an opening line that gains attention, I begin the class by saying, "Your parents are better at sex than you are." The line serves a dual purpose: it shows them the power of a great opening line, and it helps make my main point more memorable. I want to remind my students that practice is important. It makes us better. This is true about communication and sex.

The average college student is sexually active and assumes sex is a young person's activity. It's not. Bad sex is a young person's activity, but good sex often takes more time and practice than an average twenty-year-old is capable of. It might seem good to them, but it doesn't compare to what they could experience as they mature.

While young adults have youthful bodies as their advantage, older adults have multiple advantages that can make sex more enjoyable.

Experience

In his book *Outliers*, Malcolm Gladwell writes that it takes ten thousand hours to become an expert in a field.[1] While it might not take that long for sex, it does take a good amount of practice to become skilled at it. The reason parents are better at sex than their college students is because of practice. What their students may have done a few times, the parents have done a thousand times. While it might sound boring to a college student, having sex with the same person is a far better way to gain mastery of sex than having it with other people.

Trust

Sex is meant for marriage. It is more satisfying in the boundaries of a committed relationship. When you trust your partner with your life, it is easier to trust them with your body, desires, and vulnerabilities. The issue of trust is one of the reasons sex is a great barometer for marital satisfaction. As trust fades, so does sex. A bad sex life is rarely the reason for a bad marriage, but it is often an easy symptom to identify in the process of diagnosing marital health. If your sex life isn't good, how is your level of trust? Build the latter and the former will usually take care of itself.

Confidence

While age doesn't ensure self-confidence, it can contribute to it. Women in particular often feel more comfortable with themselves as they age. As a woman learns to accept her weaknesses and appreciate her strengths, it can have multiple benefits in the bedroom.

1. Malcolm Gladwell, *Outliers* (New York: Little, Brown, 2008), 35.

When a husband and wife gain confidence with one another, it can positively influence the sexual experience.

Opportunity

Married sex is better than non-married sex. If for no other reason, it's better because of opportunity. Have a bad experience with someone who isn't your spouse and you may not get another chance. Have a bad experience with your spouse and you should get another chance within a reasonable time. Married sex is bad on occasion, but you can accept it and make it better next time. One of the advantages of a long-lasting marriage is being able to put negative experiences in context. One bad experience does not mean every experience will be bad. If sex isn't mind-blowing tonight, it's okay because you will get a chance to do it again at another time. This takes the pressure off a married couple. You can relax without wondering how the other person is judging you.

Popular culture promotes the idea that young, unmarried sex is the best. That might be true in the movies, but it's not true in real life. Sex is best in the midst of a long-lasting relationship with two people who know and trust one another and are committed to the pleasure and satisfaction of their partner.

College students don't believe me, but they don't know what they are doing. Married sex can be far better than they imagine.

Learning Together

Being lovers is a mysterious act. At one moment our relationship can feel as though it was forever meant to be and naturally flows with an ease that cannot be explained. At other moments we can feel like aliens to one another.

Friendship and partnership should make us better lovers. As friends, we are always by each other's side. We want what is best for our spouse. We know how much we desire to be truly loved, so we give that love to our spouse. As partners, we learn to work with each other, understand each other's strengths, compensate for each other's weaknesses, and make the most out of every situation. It happens in business, parenting, running a household, and even sex.

Friendship gives us patience with one another. Partnership gives us the ability to learn and grow. When they are put together, we are better lovers because we patiently learn what our spouse needs and desires.

To become lifetime lovers, be willing to keep trying, failing, and trying again.

To become lifetime lovers, be willing to keep trying, failing, and trying again. Seasons change. What is important in one decade of life is not as important in another. The moment we stop intentionally growing toward one another, we will unintentionally begin to drift away from one another.

Desire for intimacy and sex can be the fuel that continually calls us to each other. When we commit to gain sexual satisfaction only from our spouse and reserve marriage for the ultimate place of intimacy, nature itself will continually drive us to one another.

BE INTENTIONAL

1. Of the three types of married sex—spontaneous, scheduled, and maintenance—which would you like more of in your relationship? Why?

2. Do you pursue your spouse and feel pursued by them? What makes you feel most desired?

3. If you could tell your spouse one thing about sex, what would it be?

4. How can you both grow to become better lovers?

13

How to Have Great Sex

How can we have great sex? While there isn't a single formula, there are many principles that make us better lovers.

The key to great sex is foreplay. Without it, every sexual encounter will be second rate. But foreplay is more than just what happens in the minutes before sex. It is everything that precedes the sexual encounter.

One evening, at a three-hour marriage seminar, I spoke primarily about the first section of this book—friendship. At the end of the evening the crowd submitted questions for a Q & A. One person was outraged. They wrote a lengthy introduction to their question, explaining how important sex is to marriage and how they couldn't believe I would speak for three hours and never spend a serious amount of time on the topic. After the diatribe came the question: "What do you think is the biggest misconception about sex?"

My answer? "The biggest misconception about sex is that a three-hour talk about friendship in marriage is not a direct discussion about sex."

It is foolish to attempt to segregate sex from the rest of life. The human mind doesn't work that way. And few things influence sex as much as friendship. The greatest of lovers are the best of friends.

The best thing the average couple can do to assist their sex life is to nourish their friendship. Great friends have great sex.

> *The best thing the average couple can do to assist their sex life is to nourish their friendship. Great friends have great sex.*

Yet every aspect of life influences sex. When an individual or couple contacts me about their sex life, the first request I make of them is to get a physical. Health issues can easily influence our sex lives in a negative way. Then I ask what other struggles might be happening in their relationship. As long as there isn't a physical issue, sex is rarely the problem. Because couples don't realize that everything is foreplay, they assume they have a sexual problem. Most often the issue is something else.

The Greatest Aspect of Sex

In a healthy marriage, the greatest aspect of sex is giving pleasure. Nothing epitomizes the highest ideals of marriage as much as each spouse making their own desires secondary in an attempt to give pleasure to the other—and all within the security of a committed, lifelong relationship. That's the highest ideal, but it's not the norm.

In too many relationships, sex becomes the symptom of a broken relationship. Feelings are hurt; intentions are questioned; trust is destroyed; each partner begins to look out for themselves at the expense of the other. Consider the two contrasts: In one relationship each spouse submits their own desires to the desires of the other in hopes to give pleasure. In the other relationship each spouse demands their own desires at the expense of the other in hopes to get pleasure.

Paradoxically, when each spouse attempts to give pleasure rather than seek it, they both give it and receive it. When each spouse demands to receive pleasure rather than gives it, neither gives nor receives.

Submission is risky business. Whenever we put the well-being of another above ourselves, we run the risk of someone taking advantage of us, exploiting us, or taking us for granted. It's a way of life no one should rush into. There is too much pain and evil in the world to quickly submit yourself to someone else. This type of relationship should only be pursued as trust is established and one's heart has been fully shown.

Yet no sexual relationship should exist except one built on mutual submission. This is why sex works as it's intended in marriage, but not outside of it. It's only after a person is found worthy of me devoting my entire life to them that they should become the object of my sexual desire. Once trust is built and commitments are made, a couple can pursue a relationship in which sex becomes about giving pleasure to the other.

For some, even in marriage, that's not the starting place. Often it's about sex and our own pleasure. But just as we mature and grow as friends and partners, so too we mature and grow as lovers and begin to experience the joy of bringing pleasure to our spouse.

As we begin to fulfill our spouse's desire, they can let down their guard and begin to submit their desire to ours. When both spouses make the pleasure of the other their highest goal, sex reaches a new level of intimacy and meaning. This should be the pursuit of every couple.

> *When both spouses make the pleasure of the other their highest goal, sex reaches a new level of intimacy and meaning.*

Don't worry if you aren't successful at this every time. No couple will ever fully arrive. If you think you have sex (or any aspect of marriage) figured out, something will happen to bring you back to earth. However, you can make progress. You can grow and mature in experience and understanding so that seeking the pleasure of the other is the highest goal.

Sadly, many couples never reach this level of sexual intimacy because they give up. Either they settle into a one-sided sexual relationship that ignores the pleasure of one spouse, or they devolve into a sexless marriage in which neither spouse is finding any satisfaction. This is an unacceptable outcome. Unless there is an unusual circumstance, a couple should never accept a sexless or "hardly any sex" relationship.

Notice the travesty of a sexless relationship. Not only is a spouse denied sexual pleasure, but they are also denied the greatest aspect of sex—giving pleasure to their spouse. When marriages do not focus on pleasing one another, they can only devolve into getting pleasure for self. The result is failed intimacy, selfishness, a lack of service, abuse, manipulation, and an absence of love.

But when a couple experiences the joys of pleasing one another sexually, not only does their intimacy grow, but that joy also ripples into every other area of life. It's a funny thing about sex. After sex, I'm more likely to clean the kitchen, mow the yard, or watch the kids. I don't intend to be more willing to do those things; I simply *am* more willing. The reason? Sex connects me with my wife, which causes my brain to think more about what would bring her pleasure. And sometimes my picking up the dirty clothes from around the bed brings her as much pleasure as anything that might happen in the bedroom.

While it should never be the intention, finding ways to please your spouse outside of the bedroom makes it more likely your spouse will find ways to please you in the bedroom. It's not a quid pro quo; it's simply the development of thoughtfulness and affection that influences every area of the relationship.

What Your Husband Wants from You in Bed

Wives, what does your husband want from you in bed? Nearly every couple I know fights about sex. When we are young and in love, it is impossible to imagine sex becoming a topic of tension. However, considering what sex involves, it makes perfect sense that it would be a common point of disagreement.

Nearly every couple has a partner who desires more sex and one who desires less.

Nothing we do makes us as vulnerable as what sex requires.

There is no area in which our mistakes or the abuses of others can injure us like sex.

We live in a culture that does not openly discuss or teach about sex.

We live in a culture that regularly gives the impression that everyone else is sexually satisfied.

Sex is influenced by our spiritual, emotional, physical, and mental problems.

When we consider these facts, it should never surprise us that we experience sexual tension within marriage. Whenever I speak with women, one of the most common questions I get is, "What does he want from me?"

It's a question about sex, and it's a good one. The answer is, "Different things for different men." Because of past experiences, mistakes, foolish decisions, and/or abuse, many men want different things from their wives. But if a man is healthy—emotionally, spiritually, physically—his desire is always the same. He wants one thing from you in bed. *You.* Unhindered. Unencumbered. You.

The great temptation for wives is to give only part of themselves to their husbands, and rightfully so. We are broken people living in a broken world. Everyone is tempted to protect themselves, especially when it comes to sex—particularly women. Yet marriage is designed for one man and one woman to fully know each other in the marriage bed.

This can't happen on the honeymoon. It takes time, effort, the building of trust, exploring vulnerabilities, learning to let go, and appreciating who God made you each to be both as a person and as a man or woman. It's a journey full of failure and success. It's such a personal journey that it should only take place in marriage. It's too risky to attempt this process outside of the vows of commitment.

This is what a man wants—at least a healthy man. Unhealthy men might be motivated by other things. But healthy men simply want *you*.

Ask yourself the following questions:

1. *Is your husband reasonably healthy?* No one is perfect. We are all broken in some ways. While his desires might not be the same as yours, are they unhealthy or just different? Is he fully committed to you? Is he faithful in a variety of areas as your husband? Is he growing emotionally, spiritually, and relationally?

2. *Are you giving him all of yourself?* Are you holding back? Are you simply giving him part of you? Are you protecting your heart or soul out of fear or uneasiness? Are you hoping to do the minimum required? Or are you giving him the best you, the most energetic you, the most engaged you? Are you seeking to find satisfaction for yourself and your spouse?

If the answer to either of these primary questions is "no," the two of you need to get help. If your husband isn't healthy, you as his wife cannot trust him with your heart. He must begin to heal before you can give yourself to him. But if your husband is healthy and you aren't giving him all of yourself, you need to get help. Explore what is holding you back, and take steps in giving your husband what he deserves—you.

Two Habits of Good Lovers

Good lovers consistently do two things outside of the bedroom that greatly influence what takes place inside the bedroom. They make frequent eye contact and routinely touch each other in a nonsexual way.

Unhealthy couples stop looking each other in the eye. Maybe it is shame. Maybe it is a feeling of contempt. Rarely is it a conscious decision. It just happens.

Regularly look each other in the eye. Doing so shows full attention when your spouse is speaking. It helps to ensure you understand what is happening in your spouse's life. Communicate with just your eyes in crowded places. It is a reminder to your spouse that they are not alone—that someone is on their side, has their back, and sees them.

It is easy to forget the power of looking each other in the eye, but on occasion life will force the action and remind me of its effectiveness. Every time Jenny and I play a card game in which we are partners, I remember the power of eye contact. We can't tell each other what cards we hold, but we work hard to read each other's eyes.

Good lovers also touch each other far more often than the average couple. Yet the touch isn't just sexual; it can also be a nonsexual touch that communicates love, support, and the simple message "I'm here for you."

A wise spouse will intentionally touch their spouse every time they are near. Instead of stepping completely out of the way as you pass, gently touch each other. Hands should be drawn to one another. A simple touch as you sit together in a booth or in a car or on the couch can serve as a great reminder that you're thinking of each other.

Touch is so powerful that it serves as a dangerous line for an inappropriate relationship. When two people who should not have a sexual relationship intentionally touch, they are on the fast track to crossing the ultimate line.

What can be used to hurt some relationships can be used to strengthen a marriage. Couples, especially men, can easily get out of the habit of touching except for sexual intent. But both sexes respond positively to nonsexual touch. Take one week and intentionally touch each other as many times as possible—make contact every time you pass one another, give a simple kiss whenever one leaves the house, hold hands while walking or watching TV. You'll soon recognize the power of a simple touch.

While nonsexual touch is intended to communicate love without sexual intent, it deeply influences sexual encounters. Frequent nonsexual touch enhances sexual touch.

Learn How to Spice Up Your Marriage from an Adulterer

When people talk to me after an affair, I rarely hear them say the sex was bad. In nearly every case, the sex in an affair is great.

Nothing else is great—the lies, guilt, broken relationships, or ruined reputation. Yet the sex is. And how can it not be? It's secretive, new, and adventurous. But great sex is not saved for adultery.

Ironically, many of the things that make adulterous sex great result from simple changes in our routine—and can be used to make married sex great.

Change in Location

Just a change in location can make the experience better. While a married couple should never risk illegal activity (e.g., don't have sex in a public park), they can make an effort to have sex somewhere other than their bedroom. When was the last time you did that?

Daytime Sex

Most married couples get in a rut of having sex in the same place and at the same time. Generally, it is either the first or the last thing of the day. What about a rendezvous at other times to make things more interesting? What about a quickie, which is an important part of any sexual relationship? When was the last time you called your spouse for a lunch date at home?

Flirting

Probably the most overlooked yet effective tool a married couple can use to spice up their sex life is flirting. Text messages, voice mails, emails, secret touches, and long gazes—all those are great ways to flirt with your spouse. Part of this communication should be about anticipating the next encounter. When was the last time you whispered in your spouse's ear while in a crowded room?

Different Positions

I'm not sure why having an affair causes people to try things they normally wouldn't, but I've sat through a number of uncomfortable conversations and heard one spouse say to the other, "But you would never try that with me." Here is a definition of a sexual rut: having sex at the same time, in the same place, the same way nearly every time. If you are in a rut, change it up. Try something new. It might not be enjoyable, but it will communicate to your spouse you are willing to try. When was the last time you tried something new or revisited something from the past?

Initiative

Maybe you never initiate sex; maybe he is never romantic. It's time to take "never" out of the sentence and start coming up with new ideas. Showing this initiative at home will often help prevent the need for you to show it elsewhere. When was the last time you went out of your way to initiate something with your spouse?

Sex in an affair may be good, but it's not the best. The best sex happens in the midst of a committed, loving relationship over the course of a lifetime. However, this relationship takes work to maintain, and whenever we find ourselves in a rut, we need to do something about it.

There are not many things a married couple would want to emulate from those having an affair. But there are some things married couples should be doing and are not. By putting more energy into our married relationship, we can often prevent the desire for any other relationship.

How to Jump-Start Your Sex Life

When a couple desires to improve their sex life, one of the best exercises they can do is to take a purposed time of seclusion away from family and friends to focus on their physical relationship.

The best sex happens in the midst of a committed, loving relationship over the course of a lifetime.

Most marriages begin with a honeymoon. Consider a couple waiting until marriage to experience the fullness of a physical relationship. After the ceremony, the groom whisks the bride away to a remote location where they establish an intimate relationship. The trip is not all about sex, but sex is by no means secondary. A couple leaves friends, families, and normal day-to-day expectations so they can focus on one another and freely connect on a deep level. Being away can create a more comfortable climate to explore the fullness of a sexual relationship.

This is a great way to start a marriage. It is also a great way to reinvigorate a marriage. When the routine of life and the pressures of raising a family begin to erode a couple's intimacy, they need to take a "sexcation." They need a time in which they are removed from friends, families, and the day-to-day expectations so they can focus on reconnecting on a physical level. The time shouldn't be all about sex, but sex cannot be secondary.

Sitting in a restaurant, I overheard two women talking about an upcoming vacation. One of them said, "I hope he doesn't expect sex every day." Obviously I don't know the woman's story and it would be unfair to judge, but I did wonder, *Is there ever a time when he should expect sex every day? What would be wrong with expecting a high number of sexual encounters for a specific time? Does she ever give him what he wants?*

For some couples, any vacation will accomplish the goal of reconnecting in an intimate way. But for other couples, one of the spouses may not be as open to that, so a specific time needs to be planned. Not every vacation has to place a high value on sex, but there should be an occasional time in which a couple breaks from the routine of life to put a primary focus on their physical relationship.

Stop and consider: how does that thought make you feel?

If it excites you, call your spouse. If they feel the same way, start making plans to get away and enjoy one another. You don't need an expensive location. The trip doesn't have to be elaborate. It doesn't have to last for a week. Just find a time, a place, and people to cover your normal responsibilities, and go have fun.

If it's acceptable to you, find out how your spouse feels about it. If they are excited about the idea, then you should follow the same path as the previous point.

If it exhausts you, that's understandable. Life is difficult enough; many people (especially women) cannot stand the thought of another expectation. Some spouses who have a lower sex drive do everything they can to keep their spouse satisfied, and making more effort can feel overwhelming. What you feel is reasonable, but if your spouse desires an extended time away, you should strongly consider it.

If it sickens you, there is a problem. Something beyond sex is wrong with the relationship. Maybe there is a lack of trust. Maybe other needs have gone unmet, so the idea of meeting your spouse's needs is exhausting. Maybe you have never properly communicated about the issue. Maybe there is personal shame or guilt that sex brings to the surface. Maybe you have an inappropriate view of sex. Whatever it might be, if the thought of a few days alone with your spouse to focus on your physical relationship repulses you, something is wrong and you need to get help to fix it.

One warning: a sexcation is a good idea for a moderately healthy couple who could use some time alone to rekindle their physical intimacy. It's not advisable for a couple who is deeply struggling with their marriage. A couple in trouble should seek counseling, but after significant improvements have been made, a sexcation can spur on even more growth.

BE INTENTIONAL

1. Everything is foreplay. What can your spouse do outside the bedroom to better your experience inside the bedroom?

2. How can you increase the number of times per day in which you touch your spouse in a nonsexual way and look them in the eye?

3. Of the five suggestions—change in location, daytime sex, flirting, different positions, and initiative—which do you desire most from your spouse? Which does your spouse need most from you? How can you make that happen?

4. What is preventing you from making the giving of pleasure the greatest aspect of your sex life?

5. Where (and when) can you go to spend some meaningful time to get your sexual relationship back on track?

14

The Twenty-Four-Hour Rule (and Other Solutions to Common Sex Problems)

One of the problems with two of the three types of sex every married couple should have is that sometimes one spouse is not in the mood.

Whether someone wants to be spontaneous or a romantic encounter has been on the calendar for a week, there are times when one person wants sex and the other does not. These times can cause great frustration within a relationship. One spouse can feel rejected, the other can feel pressured. Neither is the desired outcome. To help couples with this common frustration, I encourage implementing the twenty-four-hour rule.

This rule states that a spouse is free to turn down their spouse's initiation of sex or to cancel planned sex for whatever reason they wish, but they must initiate sex within twenty-four hours.

Got a headache? Too tired? The house too messy? The game too close? Just don't feel like it?

A spouse can turn down sex for whatever reason they wish; however, sex is a vital aspect of marriage. It is so important that if a spouse chooses to turn it down, they need a plan for the next encounter—and they need to initiate that encounter.

Consider the benefits of the twenty-four-hour rule:

It frees us from pressure. Sex should not be the result of pressure or coercion. While a healthy sexual relationship demands discipline and all discipline means sometimes doing things we don't feel like doing, we should always be free to say no to sex. Twenty-four hours gives us an opportunity to get ready and excited about it.

It gives hope. How many spouses have wondered to themselves or said out loud, "Are we ever going to have sex again?" The problem with being turned down for sex is rarely about missing the event that night; it is far more about wondering when it is going to happen next. By communicating a time frame, a spouse indicates they are turning down sex for the moment, not forever. And it gives relief to the other spouse, who can know sex will happen soon.

It communicates expectations. One of the problems with being turned down for sex is it makes one less likely to initiate again. When a couple has gone some time without sex, they can get in a strange dance where both are afraid to initiate sex and to ask what the other one desires. The twenty-four-hour rule eliminates the confusion.

No rule can solve every problem, and this rule will not be a quick fix to everything. However, it can help. The simplicity of it offers great freedom.

When You Are Too Tired for Sex

The most common phrase I hear from couples regarding sex is, "I'm just too tired."

Most people understand the importance of a healthy sexual relationship within a marriage. It isn't everything, but it is vital. On occasion one spouse will exaggerate its value, believing it is the primary aspect of marriage. More often one spouse will significantly downplay the role of sex, believing it is a sign of weakness or lack of self-control. But most people understand the meaning of sex in marriage. Still, knowing sex is important and making it important are two separate things.

Knowing sex is important and making it important are two separate things.

With all the demands of life, it is very easy for sex to be pushed to the bottom of the list. There is always "later" or "tomorrow" when it comes to making time for intimacy. Early in a marriage, this is rarely a problem. With fewer demands for newlyweds, pushing sex to the end of the day isn't an issue.

Yet as demands increase, late-night sex can become an issue. One of the biggest mistakes couples make is getting into a rut of having sex only at night. A habit that can begin in young adulthood without any consequences can become taxing as a marriage matures. If the only time a couple has sex is at night, their sexual health will suffer in the seasons of raising children and advancing careers.

Nothing can prepare a couple for how exhausting raising children can be. I often laugh as I visit new parents in the delivery wing of a hospital. Oftentimes the new father will say to me, "If we can just get through these next six weeks of no sleep, we'll be good." I always want to say, "Six weeks? How about sixteen years?" No doubt the newborn stage has unique sleep challenges, but sleep is never the same after a baby is born. With each child added, life becomes more complex, and parents spend most of their lives in desperate need of a nap.

For many couples, as the children begin to grow, so do their careers. Family demands and work expectations both increase.

The weariness can sometimes be overwhelming. This exhaustion kills a couple's sex drive—and oftentimes their sex life—unless serious attention and intention are brought into play. If the only time a couple has sex is at the end of the day, they likely will not be having much sex.

Here is a simple solution to that problem: take every opportunity to have sex at a time other than the end of the day. It takes effort, planning, and often a change of mindset, but if you will find other times of intimacy, your relationship has a much better chance to flourish.

> *Take every opportunity to have sex at a time other than the end of the day.*

This doesn't exclude sex at night. Nighttime sex might continue to be the mainstay of a sexual diet, but if a couple can add in intimacy at other times, it will greatly enhance their experience.

The problem with having sex only at night is you continually give yourself to your spouse when you have the least amount of energy. I would never accept this of a teammate, co-worker, or friend. I would want more. As a spouse, I want more. While we partner together through life, I'm fully aware there are seasons in which my only interaction with my wife (communication, quality time, and/or sex) will be at the end of the day when we are both exhausted. That's part of life. But if that's the only time we interact, something will be missing.

By creating additional times in which we can be together, we are making sure our spouse sees us at our most energized. Why should our workplace get us when we are most awake, but not our spouse?

Whether it's before kids wake up, at lunch, during naptime, after work, or during a midmorning "meeting," use your creativity. For some it will require a drastic change of mindset. And it might involve some risk—what if the kids wake up? But any energy spent in trying to find different times to have sex will be well worth it.

Not only will you have more energy to have sex, but this will tell your spouse that they are not the last thing on your daily list. It will also add variety and change to your sexual experience.

Are you too tired for sex? Then don't have sex tonight. Go to sleep, but plan on having lunch at home tomorrow and picking up something to eat on the way back to work.

When She Wants It More Than Him

Sometimes I receive comments or emails from women asking, "What do I do when my husband doesn't want as much sex as me?"

It's generally true—most men have a higher sex drive than women. I see it as I walk with couples in the months before their wedding. In almost twenty years of officiating weddings, I've yet to come across a young bride more excited about the honeymoon than the groom. I see it when dealing with couples experiencing marital dissatisfaction. When sex is a problem, it is the husband who often complains of lack of frequency. I see it in studies and statistics. But sometimes women have higher sex drives.

Far more often than some might expect, I hear from women who are unhappy with the lack of sex in their marriage. They are willing, but their partner does not have as much desire. While this is difficult in any relationship, it can be very damaging for a woman.

She reads blog posts encouraging wives to have more sex with their husband and wonders what is wrong with her. She hears sermons joking about the traditional sex roles and assumes she must not be attractive or desirable. She listens to her friends complain about their husbands' sexual desires and quietly wishes she had the same problem.

When a husband has a higher sex drive that is unsatisfied, it is not a pleasant situation, but it doesn't attack his sense of worth as a man. As a matter of fact, it might make him feel more like a man because of the perception that men always want sex.

When a wife has a higher sex drive that is unsatisfied, it can attack the very core of who she is as a woman. Is she beautiful? Is she attractive? Does she have value? Is she wanted?

Yet rarely does a man's low sex drive have much to do with his wife. In a majority of cases, it falls into one of the following four categories:

1. *Difference in sex drive.* Rarely do spouses have a similar sex drive. And about 30 percent of the time—that's three in ten women—the wife has a higher drive than her husband. In this case, the husband should make a concerted effort to please his wife. They should communicate, negotiate, and find a common ground where both partners feel heard, understood, and appreciated. A general rule is a couple should have a lot more sex than one partner wants and a little less than the other wants. If the couple can't find a middle ground, they should be quick to seek help from a marriage counselor.

2. *Health issues.* Many health issues first become symptomatic in the realm of sex. Low testosterone, high blood pressure, ED, and a plethora of other issues can hurt a man's sex drive. As I said in the previous chapter, the first piece of advice I give to any couple I see is to get a physical examination. Learning the cause of a low sex drive is the first step. This can bring relief to the wife and give the husband an opportunity to do something about the problem. Most men could improve their sexual desire with a simple exercise plan and better eating.

3. *Addiction.* Any addiction can hurt sexual function, but the three most common ones I see that hurt sex drive in men are smoking, alcoholism, and pornography. In general terms, smoking kills the ability, alcoholism kills the desire, and pornography displaces the act. In all three cases, the addiction is having a negative effect on the wife. Most of the time the men deny that their actions are creating a problem, because they don't want to do anything about it. When an addiction

is causing negative consequences for others, it must be confronted. Our wives must take priority over cigarettes, a drink, or any other temptation we might face.

4. *Adultery.* When a low sex drive can't fit into any of the three previous categories, it can often be explained by adultery. When a man is having an affair, he often has just enough sex at home to keep suspicions at bay. The thrill of the forbidden sexual escapade is always more exciting than the traditional sexual relationship, so he trades the exciting for the mundane. It's fun at the beginning but devastating in the end.

Obviously, the most important element in dealing with this issue is diagnosing it properly. If your husband has medical issues and you accuse him of having an affair, things will not go well. If he's having an affair and you just assume it's a lower sex drive, deception will kill the relationship.

The key to solving this conflict is the same for every conflict—open, honest communication and a willingness to take action. Discuss the concerns at play. Get a physical to rule out any medical issues. See a marriage counselor for tips and insights. Whatever you do, do not ignore the issue.

In marriage, if an issue is important to one spouse, it is important to both spouses. If one spouse is feeling frustrated, both spouses should work to ease that.

When Kids Ruin the Moment

There are two serious threats to my marriage bed. They aren't the only threats, but they are the primary threats. And they have names—Ella and Silas.

If it was left to them, they would sleep in my bed every night. And who can blame them?

It happens often, especially in the winter. I will put my children to bed and think, *I feel sorry for them that they have to sleep alone.*

Few things are better than sleeping (yes, actually sleeping) next to someone. If you are cold, you have a built-in heater. If you are lonely, you have a friend. If you are afraid, you have someone to comfort you.

Studies have shown that few things calm our minds and prepare our bodies for sleep like physical contact with another person as we go to bed. I can't blame my kids for wanting to sleep in their parents' bed, but I don't allow them to.

The parenting advice can be debated. Is it better for the kids to learn to sleep in their own bed, or does the attachment with their parents outweigh independence? My guess is that for the child, it doesn't really matter. Some kids will do better in their own bed while other kids will do better in proximity to their parents.

But the marriage advice is clearer. It's better for the marriage when kids sleep in their own bed.

It's not always easier. Often it is easier not to fight the battle—to throw the kids in bed, deal with sleeping on 1 percent of the bed, and do your best. But while it's easier in the moment, it's harder in the long run. It would be far better to fight the initial battle in order to win the war than to continually concede to the sleeping choices of the children.

When kids are consistently allowed in their parents' bed, what do the parents have left? What space is uniquely reserved for a husband and wife? In our house, the bed belongs to the parents. The kids don't like it. The parents are often tempted to concede. But in the end it has been worth the fight.

The general rule has been that the kids sleep in their bed until morning. After 5:00 a.m., we might allow them to slide in beside us to grab another few minutes of sleep. On occasion when a child is sick or scared, they need one of us to be with them in order to sleep. In those moments, we sleep in their bed. But they do not sleep in ours.

Why? Because we must do some things to protect our marriage. We must carve out space that belongs solely to us. We must fight against people and things that might threaten our marriage. And if you don't think your kids will try to weaken your marriage, you do not understand the nature of children. At nearly every age, they will attempt to get their way by putting a wedge between Mom and Dad. As toddlers it is an actual wedge of a small human being sleeping between husband and wife. As teenagers it is a metaphorical wedge of disagreement on punishment. Guard the space or they will take it.

> *We must do some things to protect our marriage. We must carve out space that belongs solely to us.*

Children need to know they are loved. They need to be protected, comforted, and secure. Yet they also need to know the order of relationships in a healthy home. They are part of the family, but they do not run the family. They are important to their parents, but their parents will place each other above their children.

I love Ella and Silas. I love them so much that I refuse to allow them to sleep in my bed. I choose to sleep in the same bed with their mother because it will help our marriage. And anything that helps our marriage will help them.

When Television Is More Interesting

We don't have a television in our bedroom because a counselor discouraged it. I want one. I grew up with one. One of my favorite things about vacation is that most hotels or houses have one in the bedroom. But we don't have one because a counselor said we shouldn't.

The reasoning makes sense. Couples with a television in the bedroom tend to have less communication and less sex, sleep less, and eat more. For many couples, especially couples with small children, the bedroom is the only space that belongs exclusively to them. When a television invades that space, attention is turned toward it and away from each other. It's bad for marriage.

A television has no more business in a couple's bedroom than it does a child's bedroom. Yet there is a bigger issue here. While I've used the idea of TV, what I want to talk about is listening to others. We live in a dangerous time in which there is no one in our lives who can tell us to start or stop a behavior. Left to ourselves, we will fail. Yet in the wisdom of community, we have a good chance at success.

An interesting characteristic of relationships that fail is that one or both partners are unwilling to do what a professional says. I've yet to see the exception. It requires the humility to submit one's own will and to do what someone else tells you to. Whose advice are you willing to listen to and follow because they know more than you? True, not everything a counselor says is law. They can make mistakes like anyone else. Yet most marriage counselors know what they are talking about. They work with couples on a continual basis, and rarely are problems unique to one couple. Marriage counselors often hear the same thing every day. Because of this, a majority of the advice they give has been proven in multiple relationships. They aren't smarter than you; they simply have had more experience with marriage and know what works and what doesn't. When a counselor says it is unwise to do something, it is probably unwise to do it.

What is something you do for your marriage simply because it is the wise thing to do? If you are doing whatever you want, when-ever you want, your marriage is suffering. We all need restraint. Oftentimes what we want in the moment is not what is best. The ability to choose the wise action over the desire of the moment is often the difference between success and failure.

We often don't realize we are facing the choice between what we want now and what we want in the long term. In the short term, it would be nice to go to sleep while watching television. In the long term, it would be better to have my wife in bed beside me for years to come. Which wins tonight—what I want in the moment or what will most likely lead to me having what I want in the future?

If there is nothing you are doing simply for wisdom's sake today, then your marriage is probably in worse shape than you realize. The problem with ignoring wisdom is that its consequences usually aren't noticed until much later.

I doubt newlyweds have less sex or communication because of a television in the bedroom. Yet I have no doubt that is the case for a couple who has been married for ten years and has three small children. Once a television is in the bedroom, it's probably not coming out. Wisdom says never put one there, even if you think it would be okay for now.

A good marriage doesn't just happen. It takes hard work, good decisions, and a fair amount of grace. Wise couples realize they don't know it all. They seek help, heed advice, and are willing to submit their desires for the greater good. If a counselor I trust says I'll have a better sex life if I leave the TV in the living room, I'll leave the TV in the living room.

BE INTENTIONAL

1. What do you think about the twenty-four-hour rule? What is something you can negotiate regarding a common tension within your sexual relationship?

2. Of the common problems listed in this chapter, which is the most relevant to your relationship? How can you make it better?

3. How does a healthy sexual relationship between the two of you make you better parents?

4. What issues do you need to discuss with your doctor? When will you make the appointment?

Conclusion

How to Save Your Marriage

When your marriage is good and you read a book like this, you can be encouraged, take a tip or two you haven't thought about, be reminded of some things you already knew, and move on. When your marriage is bad and you read a book like this, it is often difficult to know what to do.

The good news: marriages can change. No matter what the current marital satisfaction is, a couple can dramatically improve the state of their marriage, and often in a short period of time. In just months a marriage on life support can have a steady heartbeat. I often see a marriage that was broken pieced back together and become a thriving relationship.

The bad news: marriages can change only if both parties are willing. It takes two people to make a marriage work, but it only takes one person to destroy it. If your spouse is not willing to do the work necessary to have a successful marriage, there is nothing you can do about it.

Yet if both parties are willing, a marriage can radically change.

Across from my desk are a couch, a coffee table, and two blue chairs. Without much thought, I can look at that small seating area and list twenty couples whose marriages were over as one or both spouses were seated near that coffee table and I listened to what was going on. For some there had been an affair, for others years of apathy, and for a few others there was so little emotion in the room you would think the two people were total strangers. In most situations I can tell the state of the marriage by how and where people sit. I meet them at the door, and they sit as I'm shutting the door. When they sit on the couch and she puts a pillow between them, I can tell they are in trouble. When they sit on opposite ends of the couch and turn away from one another, I know they have issues. When they both sit in the blue chairs and I'm left on the couch, I assume the anger is nearly overwhelming.

I can look across my desk and still see the couples. I've wept with people in the darkest moments. I've been saddened by the choices of husbands or wives.

But I can also see so many couples whose marriages were done and yet, all these years later, are fully alive. The couples aren't perfect, but their relationships are so much healthier than when I first saw them.

The benefit of not being a counselor is that my relationship with couples is not counselor/client. While there are limitations on how I can help them, there are not many limitations on how I can relate to them. I stay in their lives whether their marriage makes it or not. I see the outcomes beyond the immediate "stay together or divorce" decision.

I see their kids. The happy, healthy, innocent children who have no idea how close they were to living in two homes with parents who weren't married. I interact with the couples' parents, some who have a slight insight into the trouble that occurred and others who will never know the struggle their children endured. I see the couples years removed from their darkest day and now thriving in a meaningful relationship.

With all confidence I can say this: a couple will never regret fighting for their marriage. If both partners fully engage in the process and are willing to do whatever it takes to make a marriage work, they will forever be grateful for what they learn, experience, and become.

Two Roads

The image I use with couples is that of two roads. Whenever they face a difficult time, they have one of two roads to choose. (See Matthew 7:13–14.)

The first road looks easy. It is the path we are all tempted to take. The crowd always takes this road. It is wide, well paved, and the obvious choice. But if you follow that road for a while, you will notice it begins to narrow, the path gets less smooth, and the easy way becomes very difficult.

The second road looks hard. It is the path we are all tempted to avoid. There is never a crowd on this second road. It is narrow, rocky, dark, and one that no one would ever choose to take on their own. But if you follow that road for a while, you will notice that over time, it begins to widen, the rocks begin to disappear, and the hard ways become much easier.

It's no wonder so many people choose what they do. In the immediate moment the choice seems obvious. But if you speak with someone who has traveled both roads (or in my case, walked alongside others who are traveling those roads), you will hear that the obvious choice isn't always the right one.

When a couple goes through a rough time, the easy road is to end the relationship. I'm not saying divorce is easy, but it often seems much easier than doing all the work necessary to keep the relationship going. The easy road requires no reflection, no introspection, and no need to learn anything. The common thought is, *I'll end this, take some time off, and find someone else.* But divorce is never easy. Give it some time and what appears easy in the moment becomes very difficult.

The hard road is intimidating for everyone. If the marriage is truly broken, it seems useless for an individual to do what's necessary to save it because they don't know if it can be saved. "What if I do all of this and we still get divorced?" they ask. I understand the question. Yet if they will make the choice, do the work, and walk the hard path, they can not only save the marriage but radically transform it.

I often tell couples, "I'm not asking you to rescue this marriage. I'm asking you to work to establish a marriage you have never known or experienced. If you are willing to do this, your marriage can be so much better than you could ever imagine, but if you give up now, you will never know what could have been."

> I often tell couples, "I'm not asking you to rescue this marriage. I'm asking you to work to establish a marriage you have never known or experienced."

My job in those moments as a marriage triage nurse is not just to point the couple in the direction of their specialist; it's also to encourage the belief that they can still live. Some don't believe me. Despite my pleading, they walk away. I spend the weeks and years afterward attempting to assist them in forming a new life, sometimes alone and sometimes with a new partner.

But some do believe me. They refuse to give up, and they do the work. It often gets worse before it gets better. Maybe for the first two weeks they experience a euphoria of hope, but eventually the work gets tough, the counseling sessions get personal, and each individual is confronted with their personal failures and needs. It can get ugly. But if they stick it out and keep doing what they are told, eventually the relationship begins to turn.

I can look across my desk and see those couples. The moment their relationship was teetering on the edge is right before my eyes. But even as I see them then, I can see them now—laughing, committed, able to communicate, friends, partners, and lovers.

When your relationship is on the brink, you have to choose one of two roads. Be intentional and choose the hard road.

Five Keys to Save Your Marriage

Saving a marriage takes a mindset. Beyond the need for both parties to engage, five qualities are vital if you want to make it. I consider them prerequisites. No matter what marriage problems might present themselves, when these characteristics are present, the issues can be overcome. While all five are not necessary at the first meeting, they are vital in the early stages. When even one of these characteristics does not quickly appear, the marriage is in great danger.

1. *Humility.* There is really only one enemy of marriage, and that is pride. When pride goes unchecked, a healthy marriage cannot exist. Humility gives us the ability to recognize our mistakes, admit our faults, seek help from others, forgive, and seek forgiveness. Humility is the foundation upon which every healthy marriage is built. It is the most important quality needed to save your marriage.

2. *Respect.* It is difficult to respect someone who has hurt you. Normally when a marriage struggles, some aspect of respect has been lost. However, there is a vast difference between not being able to respect what a person has done and not being able to respect any part of the person. Even if you don't respect something your spouse has done, they still deserve some level of basic human dignity. Even if you don't respect them as a husband or wife, being able to find some area in which you do respect them (for their parenting, their talents, the work they do, etc.) can go a long way toward rebuilding respect for them as a spouse. Respect is always easier to expand than to create. When it is totally lost, it is very

difficult to rebuild. If you can salvage respect, you can save your marriage.

3. *Mercy.* Rarely does mercy have anything to do with the person to whom we need to give mercy. It most often is defined by our own understanding of how much we need it. Mercy is directly tied to humility. As pride grows, our understanding of our need for mercy diminishes. The less we think we need mercy, the less mercy we give to others. Problems in a marriage cannot be solved without the giving and receiving of mercy.

4. *Communication.* Marriages cannot be saved without communication. While ignoring problems might give the appearance of peace, true peace is only found when we talk through the serious issues. If communication stops, the marriage suffocates because communication is the oxygen it needs. A key to marriage is not agreeing on every issue but communicating about every issue—feeling heard and understood, and having the ability to reapproach a topic if conditions change. Where communication is present, problems can be solved.

5. *Resilience.* I love the phrase "We will do whatever it takes." I often ask couples to write it down, place it where they will both see it, and believe it. Changing a marriage is not easy. It is deeply personal. It will challenge you in every way imaginable. Yet it is possible. And the greatest threat to a marriage is one partner giving up. As long as a couple has resilience, they still have a chance no matter how bleak the circumstances may look.

Contrarian Advice: Don't Chase Your Spouse

Too often when a husband runs from his responsibility, the wife chases him. Terrified of what she might lose, she runs after him, begging him to turn around. Ironically, her actions can enable his behavior. Instead of experiencing the consequences of his decision, he is able to try freedom while keeping the comforts of home. Instead of being forced to make a decision, he can continue going the direction he is headed without any loss.

Instead of chasing a running husband, a wife should set her boundaries. She needs to make it very clear who she is, where she is, and where she will be. She should communicate her desire for her husband, her desire to work on their marriage, and her refusal to chase after him. She should draw her lines in the sand and make it clear she will not cross them.

She will not live with someone who is having intimate conversations with other people. She will not be married to someone who continues to sleep with other people. She is going to counseling with or without her husband.

These and other boundaries should be communicated clearly.

Standing one's ground seems counterintuitive when a spouse runs, and it never guarantees a positive outcome. However, it is a much wiser choice than chasing after someone. If you chase them, they will run. If you don't, they will be forced to decide what they want.

When my dog runs, I don't chase her. Every time I turn the other way, she turns around and comes to me. But my dog is trained and loving; not every man is that way. However, some are. If he runs, don't chase him.

When You Say, "I Never Loved You"

"I never loved you," he says. There's another woman. He's not ashamed. The marriage is ending and he believes he never loved the woman he married years ago.

"I never loved you," she says. Her heart is dead. She's unmoved. The marriage ended years ago in her mind. Nothing but a piece of paper and the public perception still remains of a love that she now believes never existed.

"I never loved her." "I never loved him." I hear it on a near weekly basis. It could make me wonder what was happening five, ten, or thirty years ago when the wedding was taking place.

To my knowledge, I've never performed a wedding ceremony for two people who didn't love each other. Who married these people? How did they not notice the absence of love? The truth is, very few couples get married without love. Sure, it happens. There is social pressure to marry or the delusion that a certificate will force feelings that aren't there. No doubt it happens, but it is rare.

So why do so many couples who are divorcing say they never loved each other? It could be a defense mechanism. As a way to justify what they're doing, they say it in hopes people will understand the decisions they're making.

Yet far more often, it's not a lie they're telling others; it's a lie they're telling themselves. When a couple sits in my office and one says, "I never loved him/her," my common response is, "I don't believe you." I know they believe it, but I don't believe it's true.

Humanity has an amazing ability to rewrite history. You thought Vanilla Ice was cool. History proved he wasn't. You now claim to have never known him. You thought the mullet was a great haircut. The pictures prove it wasn't. You now claim your mother made you do it.

As time passes, we revise history to make sense of our current feelings. What we don't realize is that our current feelings dictate our understanding of the past more than our past dictates our current feelings. What was your marriage like a year ago, five years ago, ten years ago? How much did you love your spouse when you got married? What was your dating relationship like?

Your answers to those questions reveal more about the state of your relationship today than the state of your relationship back then. We view our past through the lens of our present. We always revise history.

So when a couple comes to me with a broken marriage and one says, "I never loved him/her," I know it is not true. And I know those feelings can change.

In the same way that a couple can go from being deeply in love at the altar to believing they were never in love, they can also go from not feeling any love to feeling deep amounts of affection. The truth is, we control our feelings. Therefore we can redevelop the feelings we have lost. A marriage that feels loveless is not hopeless. Genuine feelings can be rekindled. It takes time, energy, and effort. It may not be easy. Yet it is always worth it.

We view our past through the lens of our present. We always revise history.

If you are to the point that you no longer feel love for your spouse, this redevelopment needs to happen under the direction of a professional counselor. If you want to test my theory that the feeling of love can be developed, try one or all of the following:

Revisit the site of your first date and share your thoughts and feelings from that night.

Read old love letters to one another.

Tell each other when you first felt love for the other and why.

Unplug from all technology, take a walk, and discuss your favorite moments from marriage.

Find your favorite picture—past or present—of your spouse, show it to them, and explain why it's your favorite.

Feelings come and go. They can be regained just as easily as they can be lost. If you have lost the feeling of love, redevelop it. If you still have the feeling, work hard not to lose it. But whatever you do, don't assume that what you feel now is what you have always felt or will always feel.

How Your Marriage Can Start Changing

Your marriage can begin changing today. It's not easy or painless, but it's possible. Yet there is only one way for this to happen. It's not by getting your spouse into counseling, finding a way to change them, or getting your way.

You can't change your marriage by changing your spouse because you can't change your spouse. If you think you can, stop it. If you are trying, stop it. If you still doubt me, stop it. You can't change your spouse. But you can change you.

You can pray for your spouse to change, but you can only work toward your own change. Both spouses must be involved to save a marriage, but you can start with yourself.

Here are eight questions to ask yourself regarding your marriage:

1. *Am I full of pride?* Pride can express itself not only with an arrogant demeanor but also as self-loathing. "Look at me" and "poor me" are the same phrase with different wording.

2. *Am I expecting too much?* Marriage is not supposed to complete you. Your spouse is incapable of making all your dreams come true. Marriage is a difficult struggle that reminds you heaven is not found on earth. To expect it from others is to expect too much.

3. *Am I being too aggressive or too apathetic?* Forcing your way or never communicating your way is wrong. A middle ground between apathy and aggression must be found for a marriage to be successful.

4. *Am I desiring the wrong things?* Appearance, money, comfort, and success can all be good things, but they are not the ultimate things that should be sought. Better pursuits are the desire to help others, to love well, and to seek to bring glory to God.

5. *Am I withholding mercy from my spouse?* Consider whether you give mercy to your spouse or make them earn it. When mercy becomes a transactional exchange, it is not true mercy. Without mercy, intimacy cannot flourish.

6. *Am I blinded by sin?* Addictions, pride, and obsessions can blind us to the truth. Deception is a dangerous game that

destroys relationships by destroying individuals. If there is a rebellious area of your life, it will affect your marriage. If you are in denial in one area of life, you cannot see your marriage clearly.

7. *Am I unwilling to compromise?* Marriage is one compromise after another. If you are not willing to give and take in a variety of areas, you are not willing to do what is necessary to be happy. Only in a marriage where both spouses feel as though they are giving more than the other is an actual balance of compromise taking place.

8. *Am I overly concerned about comfort?* Marriage is an exclusive relationship. It creates a hard boundary between us and others. These boundaries will confuse some, hurt some, and offend some. Yet their confusion, hurt, and offense is necessary if you are honoring your spouse over all others. This can cause discomfort. When comfort is our primary goal, we can end up pleasing everyone around us at the expense of pleasing our spouse.

For every question to which you answered yes, you have an area where change can take place.

BE INTENTIONAL

1. Are you willing to do the work necessary to make your marriage thrive? Why or why not?
2. Of the five keys to save your marriage, which one do you struggle with the most? Why?
3. Have you rewritten your history? If so, how can you look at your past through a more positive lens?
4. Of the eight questions above, which one do you find most meaningful? Which one speaks the most to your spouse?

Afterword

Whenever I perform a wedding, I wear two rings. It's a form of professional courtesy. If the best man or maid of honor loses the rings, I can quickly insert my rings and keep the wedding going.

On my left hand is the ring my wife gave me when we married. As she made promises to me and I to her, we exchanged rings to symbolize our vows. As we did so, I had the thought that every time I touched my ring I would think about her. And so I have. No matter what is going on in my day—whether I'm on the phone with an irate church member or stressed over a decision—I touch the ring and am reminded that I'm not alone. I think of Jenny and it makes life better.

On my right hand is a ring I received from my paternal grandfather. On their first anniversary, my grandfather bought my grandmother a bracelet and a pair of earrings. When she died after many years of marriage, he had that jewelry made into a ring, which he wore every day after her death.

My grandfather died when I was a senior in high school. That morning my picture was in the paper, and as he was reading his hands began to swell—he was having a stroke. The story was told to me that he took the ring off, placed it on my picture, and eventually died.

Whenever I look at that ring, I'm reminded that I come from a legacy of love. What my wife and I are doing is not unique to us. We aren't the first ones trying to live a lifetime of devotion to one another. Many have gone before us and have been successful. I imagine my grandparents had good days and bad days just like anyone else, yet they found a way to make their marriage work. We want to do the same.

I'm not sure how much my wedding ring costs. If someone wanted to pawn it they could probably get $100. Yet every year that passes, the ring becomes more valuable to me because of the memories and experiences I've shared with Jenny.

I'm not sure how much my grandfather's ring would cost, but someone would have to kill me to find out. The ring has no monetary value to me because it is my only physical reminder of my grandparents and their love. In my mind it is priceless.

As I think about my marriage, I realize that we are living between two rings. The one on my left hand was given to me years ago, and every day it becomes more important. The one on my right hand is yet to be. A day will come in which either Jenny or I will die and our marriage will end.

But when that day comes, my prayer is that we will have left such a legacy of love that there will be some physical token our loved ones will desire to have to remember us by.

We come from a legacy of love, and we want to leave a legacy of love. In order to achieve that goal we must live every day between two rings. We remember the vows we made years ago, and we abide by them. We also look forward to the legacy we want to leave, and we make decisions that will enable that vision to become reality.

Marriages end when we forget the rings. They thrive when every day is spent in light of those two reminders.

Missing the Meaning of Marriage

Marriage isn't everything. It's important. It's a major thing. But it isn't everything.

We live in a day in which society is downplaying the importance of marriage. False stats are purported (hint: your chance of divorce is not 50 percent), definitions are changing, and the importance of a lifetime commitment is often mocked.

Many people undervalue marriage. This is why I spend a lot of time writing about its importance, pleading for spouses to take it seriously, and highlighting the significance of holding marriage in high regard. To undervalue marriage is to devalue spouses, downplay the destruction a bad or broken marriage causes, and destroy any possibility of a healthy relationship.

There is an equal yet opposite mistake when it comes to marriage. It is to overvalue marriage—to exalt it above what it was created to be, to expect things from it that it can never give, or to assume it is the answer to life's greatest questions or needs.

In a response to some who undervalue marriage, others overvalue it. The intention is good. Seeing the destruction that comes from broken relationships and desiring to see people live out their commitments, the church is tempted to overstate the importance of marriage. The hope is that by making marriage sound even more important than it is, people will do a better job to live out their vows.

Sadly, overvaluing marriage does not empower people to do better. It actually has an opposite effect. Instead of helping marriages, it hinders them, creating a standard that no relationship can attain.

Marriage is meant to be a deeply meaningful relationship. Yet it's not supposed to be a person's only relationship; it doesn't have to be dramatically more refreshing than every other friendship.

Marriage demands more time and energy, but it shouldn't demand all our time and energy. As friends, partners, and lovers, we give time to our spouse and support their dreams, and they support ours. And so marriage can be a tremendous source of joy and satisfaction. Yet it isn't the only source. A person can live an extremely fulfilling life having never been married. There are many advantages to the single life and many reasons why a person would choose to refuse marriage.

When I think about my seven-year-old, I hope he grows up to experience marriage and fatherhood. I hope he commits his life to being a good and faithful husband. I want him to experience a close connection with someone in the same way I do with my wife.

Yet I have more dreams for him as well. And if my hope for him to one day be married is not his desire, that would never mean his life is less than mine. It would simply mean it's different in some ways.

Marriage is a foundational part of society that many will enjoy. Those who choose to make the commitment should work diligently at the relationship and greatly appreciate the opportunity to share life with another. However, we cannot expect more from marriage than it can provide. Marriage is wonderful, but it's not everything.

I May Not Be Married Tomorrow

I might be single tomorrow. I'm not planning on it. I hope it doesn't happen. But it could. If there is any guarantee in life, it is that we do not know what might happen tomorrow. All of us are one moment away from life being flipped upside down:

> The parent of an honors student is one phone call away from being the parent of a special needs child.
>
> The successful businessperson is one situation away from being bankrupt.
>
> The perfect house is one storm away from being a pasture.

Life can change in an instant. And never does someone say, "I saw that coming."

So many times I've sat with families or individuals in emergency rooms, funeral homes, courtrooms, and their living rooms, watching them try to come to grips with a dramatic change in life. What I've seen happen to others could easily happen to me.

My marriage could end tomorrow. With one tragedy, my wife or I could be left to live this life without the other. This fact should result in one response: radical gratitude.

Because we are not promised tomorrow, we should deeply appreciate today. Today is not perfect. There are many things we are working to improve. We still have goals to accomplish, dreams to chase, and weaknesses to improve. But today is good.

And today we have each other. We have a life we love. We recognize this day as a gift, and we do not take it for granted. It's a dangerous trap to believe we have forever. We don't. No one does.

When we fail to see how fleeting this season of life is, we miss the joy and goodness of the moment.

When we fail to see how fleeting this season of life is, we miss the joy and goodness of the moment. It's so easy to long for yesterday or hope for tomorrow that we lose sight of the unique blessedness of today.

This is true in every area of life, but it is especially true in marriage. What if this was your last day to be married? What if tomorrow you or your spouse were gone? How would that change today?

Is there a grudge that would be released?

Is there a love that would be rekindled?

Is there an unsaid word that would finally be said?

Would you hold each other a little longer?

Would you make sure not to leave the house without a good-bye kiss?

Would you call or text in the middle of the day just to check in?

Would you put each other higher on the priority list?

Would you make sure nothing stands in your way of communicating your love?

We can't live every day like it's our last. It sounds appealing, but it's not realistic. We can, however, regularly remind ourselves that we are not promised tomorrow. We can pause during the hurry and stress of the average day and remember that life is fleeting, each moment is a gift, and tomorrow we may not have those who are most dear to us today.

Fifteen years ago, I stood in my in-laws' front yard before a hundred friends and wiped a tear from my eye as Jenny walked down the aisle toward me. Ten minutes later we were married, and fifteen years later I love her more than I was capable of loving her then.

We hope for another fifty or sixty years together. But a day will come when we will not be married any longer. We can deny the fact and assume life will go on forever. In so doing, we will take much for granted and miss many opportunities. We can live in despair of the fact and be depressed, because nothing in life is guaranteed. But the only wise thing to do is recognize the truth and respond to this day with radical gratitude.

That's what I feel in this moment—for my wife, for this life, for what God has given me.

Kevin A. Thompson (MDiv, Beeson Divinity School) is lead pastor at Community Bible Church, a growing multisite church with four locations in western Arkansas. Every year he meets with nearly one hundred couples with a range of needs, from premarital counseling to navigating the most serious betrayals. A marriage and parenting conference speaker, he also blogs at www.kevinathompson.com. He and his wife, Jenny, have two children and live in Fort Smith, Arkansas.

KEVIN A. THOMPSON

For more insights on *Friends, Partners, and Lovers*, join Kevin at **www.kevinathompson.com**. You will find additional articles, bonus book material, and free videos to further nourish your marriage.

Subscribe to receive Kevin's weekly articles on marriage, parenting, leadership, and life. Find information on a marriage conference near you or inquire about bringing Kevin to your next event.

WWW.KEVINATHOMPSON.COM